Using pdf files

Books Available

By the same authors:

BP558 Microsoft Works 8.0 and Works Suite 2005 explained
BP557 How did I do that.... in Windows XP*
BP550 Advanced Guide to Windows XP*
BP548 Easy PC Keyboard Shortcuts*
BP546 Microsoft Works Suite 2004 explained
BP545 Paint Shop Pro 8 explained*
BP544 Microsoft Office 2003 explained
BP538 Windows XP for beginners*
BP525 Controlling Windows XP the easy way*
BP522 Microsoft Works Suite 2002 explained
BP514 Windows XP explained*
BP513 Internet Explorer 6 and Outlook Express 6 explained*
BP512 Microsoft Access 2002 explained
BP511 Microsoft Excel 2002 explained
BP510 Microsoft Word 2002 explained
BP509 Microsoft Office XP explained
BP505 Microsoft Works Suite 2001 explained
BP498 Using Visual Basic
BP493 Windows Me explained*
BP491 Windows 2000 explained*
BP487 Quicken 2000 UK explained*
BP486 Using Linux the easy way*
BP465 Lotus SmartSuite Millennium explained
BP456 Windows 98 explained*
BP448 Lotus SmartSuite 97 explained
BP433 Your own Web site on the Internet
BP341 MS-DOS explained
BP284 Programming in QuickBASIC
BP258 Learning to Program in C

If you would like to purchase a Companion Disc for any of the listed books by the same authors, **apart from the ones marked with an asterisk**, containing the file/program listings which appear in them, then fill in the form at the back of the book and send it to Phil Oliver at the stipulated address

Using pdf files

by

P.R.M. Oliver
and
N. Kantaris

Bernard Babani (publishing) Ltd
The Grampians
Shepherds Bush Road
London W6 7NF
England
www.babanibooks.com

Please Note

Although every care has been taken with the production of this book to ensure that any projects, designs, modifications and/or programs, etc., contained herewith, operate in a correct and safe manner and also that any components specified are normally available in Great Britain, the Publishers and Author(s) do not accept responsibility in any way for the failure (including fault in design) of any project, design, modification or program to work correctly or to cause damage to any equipment that it may be connected to or used in conjunction with, or in respect of any other damage or injury that may be so caused, nor do the Publishers accept responsibility in any way for the failure to obtain specified components.

Notice is also given that if equipment that is still under warranty is modified in any way or used or connected with home-built equipment then that warranty may be void.

First Published - July 2005

British Library Cataloguing in Publication Data:

A catalogue record for this book is available from the British Library

ISBN 0 85934 555 6

Cover Design by Gregor Arthur
Printed and Bound in Great Britain by Cox & Wyman Ltd, Reading

About this Book

Anyone who spends more than an hour or two on the Internet will have encountered the icon above, and **pdf** files. Many large documents you can download are in **pdf** format. A large proportion of electronic books, or eBooks, are also produced as **pdf** files.

pdf, or **p**ortable **d**ocument **f**ormat, was first developed by Adobe in the early 1990s. It is a file format that preserves the fonts, images, graphics, and layout of a source document, regardless of the platform and application used to create or view it. **pdf** files are compact and complete, and can be shared, viewed, and printed by anyone, anywhere, using the free Adobe Reader software.

This book, *Using pdf files,* was written using a PC running Windows XP, and using Adobe Reader 7.0 and Acrobat 7.0, as well  as other **pdf** creating software, such as deskPDF. The book is meant not only for those who don't know what a **pdf** file is, but for those who are happy using them, but want to get more out of them. Maybe to even produce an eBook or two!

The material in the book is not really presented for the reader to start at the beginning and go right through to the end. An attempt has been made to follow a logical sequence, but the more experienced user can start from any section, as they have been designed to be as self-contained as possible, or use references where this was not possible. The book doesn't describe the workings of Microsoft Windows, or how to set up your computer hardware. If you need to know more about these topics, then may we suggest that you refer to our other books, also published by BERNARD BABANI (publishing) Ltd, and listed on page (ii) of this book.

The first chapter looks briefly at what **pdf** files are, what they are used for, and why they have become so popular, as shown by the fact that over 500 million copies of the Reader software have been downloaded from Adobe's Web site.

The next four chapters cover Adobe Reader fairly extensively. From the initial download and installation, to the user interface, the toolbars, and the viewing and navigation controls. Searching, printing and how to extract data from **pdf** documents is covered next, followed by a chapter on using forms, multimedia and the commenting tools. There is a chapter on using Reader to view and manage your eBooks, and another detailing all of Reader's keyboard shortcuts.

The rest of the book is really about creating **pdf** documents and eBooks with both Adobe Acrobat and other cheaper alternative software. Although Acrobat is not a requirement for creating **pdf** files, it is certainly the standard for creating and managing them. So we based this section of the book very much on Acrobat software. We did not set out, though, to produce a definitive guide to Acrobat, only to cover the features relevant to our text.

We have tried not to use too much jargon in the book, but some always creeps in, so *Using pdf files* is rounded off with a fairly extensive glossary.

Good luck with the book and we hope you enjoy reading it and coming to terms with **pdf** files and eBooks.

About the Authors

Phil Oliver graduated in Mining Engineering at Camborne School of Mines and has specialised in most aspects of surface mining technology, with a particular emphasis on computer related techniques. He has worked in Guyana, Canada, several Middle Eastern and Central Asian countries, South Africa and the United Kingdom, on such diverse projects as: the planning and management of bauxite, iron, gold and coal mines; rock excavation contracting in the UK; international mining equipment sales and international mine consulting. He later took up a lecturing position at Camborne School of Mines (then part of Exeter University) in Surface Mining and Management. He is now retired, and spends more time writing, consulting, and developing Web sites.

Noel Kantaris graduated in Electrical Engineering at Bristol University and after spending three years in the Electronics Industry in London, took up a Tutorship in Physics at the University of Queensland. Research interests in Ionospheric Physics, led to the degrees of M.E. in Electronics and Ph.D. in Physics. On return to the UK, he took up a Post-Doctoral Research Fellowship in Radio Physics at the University of Leicester, and then a lecturing position in Engineering at the Camborne School of Mines, Cornwall, (then part of Exeter University), where he was also the CSM Computing Manager. At present he is IT Director of FFC Ltd.

Acknowledgements

We would like to thank all of our friends and colleagues, for their helpful tips and suggestions which assisted us in the writing of this book.

Trademarks

Adobe, Acrobat, Acrobat Capture, Adobe Reader and **ePaper** are registered trademarks, or trademarks, of Adobe Systems Incorporated.

deskPDF is a registered trademark or trademark of Docudesk Corporation.

Jaws PDF Creator is a trademark of Global Graphics Software Ltd.

Arial and **Times New Roman** are registered trademarks of The Monotype Corporation plc.

HP and LaserJet are registered trademarks of Hewlett Packard Corporation.

Microsoft, MS-DOS and **Windows**, are either registered trademarks or trademarks of Microsoft Corporation.

Paint Shop, Paint Shop Pro and **Jasc** are either registered trademarks or trademarks of Jasc Software Inc.

All other brand and product names used in the book are recognised as trademarks, or registered trademarks, of their respective companies.

Contents

1

What are pdf Files?

If a file has the extension .**pdf** then it is almost certainly a **P**ortable **D**ocument **F**ormat file. This format, which was developed by Adobe Systems and released in mid 1993, is used to make documents in a standard and portable way.

A **pdf** document file maintains its original document formatting for both viewing and printing on most computing platforms, such as Windows, UNIX and Mac.

The **pdf** format has become the standard for the secure and reliable distribution and exchange of electronic documents and forms around the world. It is a file format that preserves the layout, fonts and images of any source document, regardless of the application and platform used to create it.

pdf files are compact and complete, and can be shared, viewed, and printed by anyone, anywhere, using the Adobe Reader software (see Chapter 2) which is available free from Adobe. According to them, more than 500 million copies of the Reader software have been distributed.

If you need to, you can convert any document to **pdf** format using either Adobe's Acrobat software or other cheaper software products, as we describe in later chapters. So anyone can distribute and exchange secure and reliable **pdf** documents. This could be by e-mail, on a Web site, or on a disc or CD.

Governments, organisations and individuals around the world have adopted **pdf** to streamline document management, increase productivity, and reduce reliance on paper. For example, **pdf** is used by the governments of the USA, UK and Germany (to name but a few) for electronic document exchange. On a much smaller scale, the content of this book will be sent to the printers in **pdf** format. The days of type setting are long gone!

Open File Specification

The **pdf** format is an open file format specification, which means it is available to anyone who wants to develop tools to create, view, or manipulate **pdf** documents. We have seen it quoted that over 1,800 organisations have developed **pdf**-based solutions. As an example, when we came to fill in our income tax return recently, we found one company offering pdf based software. It was free of charge too; maybe we will use it next year.

Adobe maintain '**pdf** Reference' information on their Web site. This provides descriptions and specifications of the **pdf** file formats they have developed. It is intended primarily for developers, to encourage the development of third-party applications, as shown in Fig. 1.1 below.

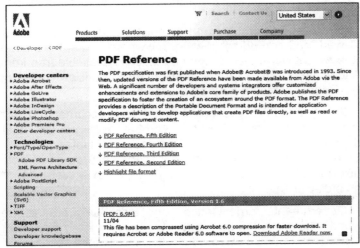

Fig. 1.1 Adobe's PDF Reference Page

If you want to look for yourself the URL address is:

http://partners.adobe.com/public/developer/pdf/index_reference.html

Some pdf File Features

pdf files are compact and fully searchable, and can be accessed at any time using Adobe Reader. As each version of the **pdf** standard comes out more features are built into the file format. Some of these include:

Navigation Features

Certain features built into the **pdf** specification allow authors to expand the usefulness of a document; for example, bookmarks, thumbnails of each page, internal and external links, form fields, article threads, buttons for navigation, notes to annotate information and views to allow a user to magnify or reduce a page to fit within the user's computer screen. **pdf** allows users to magnify up to 800% on screen with no loss of clarity. The ability to use interactive hyperlinks make **pdf** files easy to navigate. Tagged Adobe **pdf** allows text to 'reflow' for display on mobile platforms, such as Palm OS, Symbian, and Pocket PC devices.

Size and Performance

When files are viewed on a Web page, smaller is very much better as download time depends on file size. **pdf** files can be optimised to reduce their file sizes to as much as 20% of the equivalent HTML file (Hyper Text Markup Language - the usual Web page language). **pdf** can be interwoven seamlessly with HTML on a Web site, which enables authors to serve content in its most appropriate format based on the demands of content versus technology. Also, on most popular web servers there is no compression, translation or filtering penalty for using **pdf** files.

    pdf files can be 'linearised' which allows the user to start viewing the document before it is fully downloaded, much like the process used to deliver streaming video over the Internet.

Security

The **pdf** file format is very strong on data security. Authors of **pdf** files can prevent users of these files from editing, printing or copying their text and graphics content. Software developers can create their own software to read, create or modify **pdf** files without special permission or licensing. The only condition that Adobe insists on is that **pdf** security settings are respected. **pdf** documents can have special access rights applied and may be digitally signed.

Archiving with pdf Files

Many of the electronic journals and other digital resources acquired and maintained by libraries are published in **pdf** format.

As libraries grow more dependent on electronic resources, they need to consider how they can preserve these resources for the long term. Many libraries retain back runs of print journals that are over 100 years old, and which are still consulted by researchers. No digital technology has lasted nearly that long, in fact many data formats have already become obsolete. It looks at the moment as if the **pdf** format will be the one to last the course.

Some Technical Stuff

For the rest of this Chapter we go into a little more detail about the **pdf** format and how it compares with another file format you may well be familiar with - PostScript. If you want to skip to the next Chapter, feel free!

pdf is a platform-independent document format developed by Adobe as a follow-up to its PostScript language (which is now used almost universally in graphics-capable printers).

pdf vs PostScript

Perhaps we should start with basic definitions of both PostScript and **pdf**.

PostScript

PostScript is a page description language. It is a programming language, like BASIC, Fortran, or C++, like those that software engineers use to build applications. But unlike these other languages, PostScript is a programming language designed to do one thing only; to describe extremely accurately what a page looks like.

All programming languages need a processor to run their code. With PostScript, this processor is a combination of software and hardware called a Raster Image Processor (RIP), which is usually located in a printer. This RIP converts the PostScript code and renders it into dots on a page. A PostScript printer reads and interprets PostScript programs, and produces, hopefully, accurate printout on paper. If you have ever tried to print a file meant for a PostScript printer without using PostScript settings, you should remember the dozens of pages of 'rubbish' that poured from the printer. This was just the PostScipt code, but being printed as text.

An Encapsulated PostScript File, or EPS, is a PostScript program, saved as a single file that includes a low-resolution preview "encapsulated" inside it. This allows some programs to display a preview on the screen.

One common way of using PostScript is to print a file to disc, which saves it as a single PostScript file. This can then be taken to a commercial print service provider. Another, is to create EPS files as a way to save and distribute graphics.

The **pdf** format is a replacement for saved PostScript files and EPS files, but **not** a replacement for the PostScript language itself, or for the PostScript processors inside printers and other print setting machinery.

pdf - An Improved Format

pdf is a particular file format, like EPS that is built largely on the PostScript language, but it has been taken a little further. A **pdf** file not only describes pages, but can also contain information on how these pages behave and what kind of information is contained in the file. So **pdf** is a file format that is smarter than EPS, it can contain fonts, images, printing instructions, keywords for searching and indexing, interactive hyperlinks, movies, and more. But that's enough for us!

A **pdf** file is actually a PostScript file which has already been interpreted by a RIP and made into clearly defined objects. These are viewable on screen not in code, but in WYSIWYG (**W**hat **Y**ou **S**ee **I**s **W**hat **Y**ou **G**et) format for everyone to see. Because these files are already interpreted by the RIP, they should be more reliable than EPS or PostScript files when printed. Printers and print service providers can benefit from seeing the file after interpretation but before they send it to their printing devices. This means that files print faster, more accurately, and with fewer errors. As we said earlier, this book was sent to the printers as a **pdf** file.

Adobe's Acrobat program (see next Chapter) can read and print **pdf** files to non-PostScript printers by interpreting the **pdf** file into that printer's language. This is often not as reliable or as accurate as true Adobe PostScript, so professional printers usually use a PostScript processor to get optimum results.

So **pdf** is used for sending complete publications to press, for soft-proofing, for the distribution of files on the Internet, and for file archiving.

2

Adobe Reader Basics

To view **pdf** files you need to have the Adobe Acrobat Reader installed on your computer. Many new PCs will be provided with this software, but if yours isn't, don't worry, it is available as a free download from Adobe's Web site. It is also often supplied on the discs that come with most computer magazines these days.

At the time of writing, Adobe was on version 7 of the Reader. By the time you read this, there may be newer versions. This will still apply though, as new versions usually just mean extra features, mostly aimed at the heavy office Intranet users. The basics usually remain pretty constant!

System Requirements

Before going to the trouble of trying to install Adobe Reader, it may be as well to check that your computer will be up to it. If it's only a few years old, there should be no problem, but if it came from the Ark, read on. For Windows you will need:

An Intel Pentium processor, or equivalent, at least 128MB of RAM and up to 90MB of available hard disc space, Microsoft Windows 2000 with Service Pack 2, Windows XP Professional or Home Edition, or Windows XP Tablet PC Edition and Microsoft Internet Explorer 5.5 or higher.

Downloading Acrobat Reader

The Acrobat Reader program is free, and may be downloaded in the UK by going to the following page:

http://www.adobe.co.uk/products/acrobat/readstep2.html

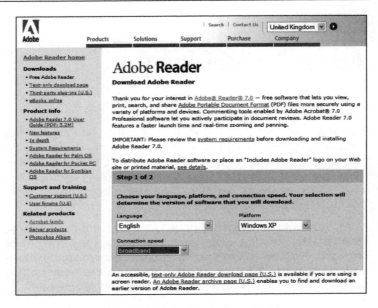

Fig. 2.1 The UK Adobe Reader Download Page

You can also get to this page by clicking the Get Adobe Reader button shown here, which appears on most Web sites that use **pdf** files, and choosing UK from the drop-down list at the top of the US page.

You will be led through easy steps that allow you to identify your language, platform, and connection speed, as shown above. We chose to download the full version of Reader (see later section), but not the Yahoo or Photoshop Album 2.0 software, and a total download of 20.3MB was indicated. No problem with a broadband connection, but with dial up you may be better buying a magazine this month! Even the basic version of Reader is a 12.6MB download!

When you are happy with the options chosen, clicking the continue button at the bottom of the page, opens the next page. Then click the download button to start the procedure. You then select a download location in the dialogue box shown in Fig. 2.2 on the facing page, and click **OK**.

Fig. 2.2 Selecting Destination

Fig. 2.3 Adobe Download Manager

The Adobe Download Manager then opens (Fig. 2.3 above) which gives you some control over the download. This is important as the file downloaded is very large. You can **Pause**, or click in the check box to **Download only when my Internet connection is idle**. It even helps you out if you lose your connection in the middle of the operation.

Fig. 2.4 Adobe Download Manager

The message box shown in Fig. 2.4 above opened the next time we switched on our PC after an abortive download. Anyway, now is the time to go and put the kettle on, or open something stronger, as the download will take a while.

Once the download is completed the Setup program automatically starts the installation on your system, as shown in Fig. 2.5 here. You don't even need to find a downloaded file and double-click it. This is

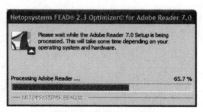

Fig. 2.5 Adobe Reader Setup

very smooth indeed, Adobe have thought it out well. A series of windows show you what is happening. You just keep clicking the **Next** button to continue, and if necessary, make changes to the offered options.

Finally, Setup should tell you it is ready to 'Install the Program'. Just click the **Install** button, then in the last window click **Finish** to exit the Setup program.

Adobe Reader Versions

As we saw earlier, there are two versions of Adobe Reader.

The basic version contains a smaller set of features to allow for fast downloading.

The full version of Adobe Reader includes the ability to search **pdf** files, play back embedded media clips, and support Digital Editions, or eBooks as they are usually called.

In this book we assume you have installed the full version of Adobe Reader. If this is not the case, you may be asked to download update features as you use the program.

Automatic Program Updates

Once you have installed Adobe Reader 7.0 it will attempt to keep itself up to date automatically. Whenever an update is available from Adobe the pop-up window shown below will open.

Fig. 2.6 A Critical Update Download

This is a very painless way to keep your program up to date, especially if you have a Broadband connection, but of course it only works if you are connected to the Internet.

Looking at Adobe Reader

If you check your Windows desktop (the opening screen before any programs are running) you should find that a new Adobe Reader button has been added, as shown here. An entry will also have been added to the end of the **start**, **All Programs** menu structure.

Double-clicking the desktop icon, or just clicking the menu option, will open an 'empty' copy of the Reader, as shown below in Fig. 2.7.

Fig. 2.7 The 'Empty' Adobe Reader Window

As no **pdf** document (or file) has been opened yet it only contains the menu and tool bars at the top of the window. To get a useful **pdf** file to view, it may be a good idea to go to the Adobe Web page:

    www.adobe.com/products/acrobat/readstep2.html

This is the US version of that shown open in Fig. 2.1 on an earlier page.

If you click the __Adobe Reader 7.0 User Guide (PDF 2.8M)__ link in the **Product info** menu on the left side of this page, the User Guide will download and be opened in your Web browser, as shown in Fig. 2.8 below.

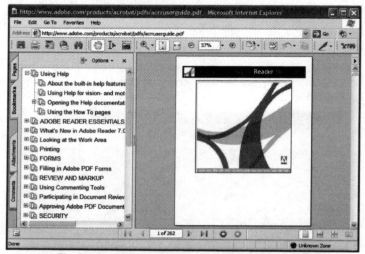

Fig. 2.8 The User Guide Open in an Explorer Window

What you have done here is opened a **pdf** file from a Web site and downloaded it to Acrobat Reader working 'inside' your Web browser. It shows how well **pdf** files can be handled over the Internet. Large files are often progressively opened in Reader as they download, so you don't have to wait until the whole file is downloaded. This didn't happen for us, though, with this file!

The 'danger' of reading **pdf**s straight from the browser is that they are only resident in your computer's memory. If you close the browser window, or move to another page, the file

is 'lost' and has to be downloaded again if you need it later on. If you will need a file again, it is always a good idea to save it to your hard disc. This is easy with Adobe Reader, just click the **Save** button, shown here, and the file will be saved in your **My Documents** folder.

The Reader Screen

The default Adobe Reader screen, or work area, is shown below. It is perhaps worth spending some time looking at the various parts that make up this screen. Adobe Reader follows the usual Windows conventions and if you are familiar with these you can skip some of this section, but even so, a few minutes might be well spent here.

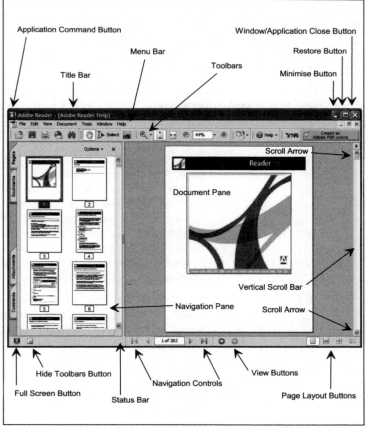

Fig. 2.9 The Adobe Reader Screen Layout

The layout as shown is in a window, but if you click on the application restore button, you can make Adobe Reader take up the full screen area available. Using a window can be useful when you are running several applications at the same time and you want to transfer between them with the mouse.

Note that in this case, the Adobe Reader window displays the Adobe Reader Help document, and has a solid 'Title bar', indicating that it is the active application window. Although multiple windows can be displayed simultaneously, you can only enter data into the active window (which will always be displayed on top unless you view them with a split screen). Title bars of non-active windows appear a lighter shade than that of the active one.

The Adobe Reader screen is divided into several areas which have the following functions:

Area	*Function*
Command button	Clicking on the command button, (see upper-left corner of the Adobe Reader window), displays a pull-down menu which can be used to control the program window. It allows you to restore, move, size, minimise, maximise, and close the window.
Title Bar	The bar at the top of a window which displays the application name and the name of the current document.
Minimise Button	When clicked on, this button minimises Adobe Reader to an icon on the Windows Taskbar.
Restore Button	When clicked on, this button restores the active

window to the position and size that was occupied before it was maximised. The restore button is then replaced by a Maximise button, as shown here, which is used to set the window to full screen size.

Close button

The extreme top right button that you click to close a window.

Menu Bar

The bar below the Title bar which allows you to choose from several menu options. Clicking on a menu item displays the pull-down menu associated with that item.

Toolbars

The bar below the Menu bar contains the Toolbars, which have buttons that give you mouse-click access to the functions most often used in the program.

Navigation Pane

Below and on the left side is a navigation pane that helps you browse through the current **pdf** document. This tabbed pane displays a document's bookmarks, page thumbnails, and articles.

Document Pane

This displays **pdf** documents, usually one page at a time.

Scroll Bars

The areas on the screen that contain scroll boxes in vertical and horizontal bars. Clicking on these bars allows you to control the part of a document which is visible on the screen.

Scroll Arrows

The arrowheads at each end of each scroll bar which you can click to scroll the screen up and

	down one line, or left and right 10% of the screen, at a time.
Status Bar	The bottom line of the document window that contains details of a document's status, and the following buttons to control how a **pdf** file is viewed.
Full Screen Button	Lets you view **pdf** pages using the entire screen; all menus, bars, and window controls are hidden.
Hide Toolbars Button	Switches on Read mode, which gives you more screen area to read pages,  but retains the menu bar, the navigation pane and a limited selection of tools on the status bar.
Navigation Controls	These provide a quick way to navigate through documents.
View Buttons	These two buttons let you move backwards and forwards through the viewing path you have used when reading a document.
Page Layout Buttons	Lets you control the page layout of the document being read. The options vary from a single page at a time (shown here) to continuous facing pages.

The Toolbars

Fig. 2.10 The
Toolbars Menu

There are ten different toolbars available in the toolbar area of Adobe Reader. To see the full list you can use the **View**, **Toolbars** menu command, or more easily, right-click in the toolbar area. Both methods open the menu shown here in Fig. 2.10. In this list active bars are shown with a tick in a blue box to their left. Clicking on a list entry will toggle that toolbar on or off. By default, only six bars are active, as shown here.

If you hold the mouse pointer over a tool button you will see the name of the tool. Holding the pointer over the gripper bar on the left edge of a toolbar will show the name of the toolbar. Not all the buttons (or icons) are visible at any one time. To see other available buttons click the toolbar options button ▼ at the right end of each bar, as shown in Fig. 2.11. Clicking any of the buttons now displayed will action that function.

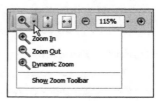

Fig. 2.11
The Zoom Toolbar

In the next section we describe the functions of the buttons on the default toolbars.

The File Toolbar

A bar of icons that you click to carry out some of the more common Reader 'housekeeping' actions, as follows:

Button   Function

 Open an existing **pdf** file.

 Save a Copy of the current document to disc with the option to use another name.

 Print - Opens the Print dialogue box so you can contol a printing operation.

 Email - Opens your default e-mail program with the current file as an attachment.

 Search - Opens the Search pane which lets you search for a word, or phrase, in the current **pdf** document, or in other **pdf** documents on disc.

The Basic Toolbar

A bar of icons that you click to open some basic Adobe Reader tools, as follows:

Button   Function

 Hand Tool - You click and drag this tool to move around a page and view all the areas of it.

 Select Tool - Used to select text (I pointer), or an image (pointer) in a **pdf** document. You can then use the Copy and Paste commands to copy the selection to another application, like a word processor.

 Snapshot Tool - Used to copy the contents of the selection (text, an image, or both) to the Clipboard or to another application. Both text and images are copied as an image.

There are some other tools, such as commenting tools, which are only available in documents that have had additional usage rights given to them by their authors. These extra tools are added to the work area, when they are available.

The Zoom Toolbar

Buttons that you click to give several methods for magnifying the view of **pdf** documents between 1% and 6,400%. With the Zoom Tool buttons, the mouse pointer changes to the tool, until another tool is selected.

Button   *Function*

 Zoom In Tool - You click this ⊕ tool on the page to make the text larger. To zoom in on a specific area, use the tool to draw a rectangle. When this tool is selected, you can hold down the **Ctrl** key while clicking or dragging to zoom out instead.

 Zoom Out Tool - You click this ⊖ tool on the page to make the text smaller and view a larger area. When this tool is selected, you can hold down the **Ctrl** key while clicking or dragging to zoom in.

 Dynamic Zoom Tool - You click this ⊕ tool in the text and then drag it, **up the screen** to zoom in to the area where you clicked, or **down** to zoom out. This tool needs playing with, to get used to it.

 Fit Page - Used to resize the page to fit entirely in the Reader document pane.

 Fit Width - Used to resize the page to fit the width of the window or document pane.

 Zoom Out - Click this button to zoom out the screen magnification to the next zoom setting.

 Zoom Menu - Click the down arrow to open a drop-down menu of specific zoom options and percentages. If you click the percentage number in the zoom box it will be highlighted, and you can then type in another specific zoom magnification %. Pressing the **Enter** key will activate it.

 Zoom In - Click this button to zoom in the screen magnification to the next zoom setting.

The Rotate View Toolbar

This toolbar contains two buttons that you can click to change the view of a page in 90-degree increments. These do not change a page's actual orientation, only how you see it in Reader.

Button   Function

 Rotate Clockwise - You click this button to rotate the current page 90 degrees in a clockwise direction.

 Rotate Counterclockwise - You click this button to rotate the current page 90 degrees in an anti-clockwise direction.

To display both these buttons at the same time in the toolbar, click the one visible button, or the triangle next to it, and choose **Expand This Button** from the drop-down menu, as shown in Fig. 2.12. To return to the normal button view, click

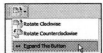
Fig. 2.12
Expanding Bars

the left-pointing arrow to the right of the expanded button.

The Help Toolbar

This toolbar contains only one button.

 Help - You click this button to open a drop-down menu of Help options, as shown in Fig. 2.13.

The **Adobe Reader Essentials** option opens a **How to..** pane to give you quick access to basic help when you start using the program. As long as you are connected to the Internet, **Online Support** opens your browser at Adobe's Reader support page.

Fig. 2.13
Help Menu

The final option, **Adobe Reader Help**, opens a detailed help system into its own window. This is discussed in the next chapter.

The Search the Internet Toolbar

This toolbar also contains only one button.

 Search the Internet using Yahoo - This button lets you search for text on the Internet, or in one or more **pdf** documents on your hard disc. It opens the Search PDF pane, as shown here in Fig. 2.14.

Fig. 2.14 The
Search PDF Pane

The options in this Search pane are all self explanatory, so we will not spend long here. If you select the **Search only in PDF files** option, as we have, you will get a listing of the **pdf** files on the Internet that the search engine Yahoo could find that contain your search word, or phrase. If you don't select this, you will get a listing of all the Web pages it could find.

The Edit Toolbar

This toolbar contains buttons that you click to carry out editing functions on comments and text in form fields.

Button   *Function*

 Spell Check - Check the spelling of any comments or form fields in the current **pdf** document.

 Undo any editing changes you have made. You can **Expand This Button** as shown in Fig. 2.12.

 Redo any editing changes you have made.

 Copy any selected text to the Windows clipboard.

Before we 'finish with' toolbars Acrobat Reader has another couple of tricks you may find useful:

To select the **Hand** tool temporarily, without deselecting the current tool, hold down the spacebar.

To select the **Zoom In** tool temporarily, press the **Ctrl** key and hold down the **spacebar**.

The Status Bar

As is usual with Windows applications, the status bar is located at the bottom of the Adobe Reader window and contains details of a document's status, and buttons to control how a **pdf** file is viewed, as shown in Fig. 2.15 below.

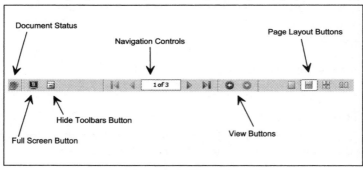

Fig. 2.15 The Adobe Reader Status Bar

Document Status

 When a document is restricted or has a special status, icons appear in the left-hand segment of the status bar.

The icon shown here indicates that the document is secure. You can double-click a document status icon to view more information.

Full Screen View

 The **Full Screen** button lets you view pdf pages using your entire screen; all menus, bars, and window controls are hidden, and the document is shown one full page at a time. This is especially useful when you settle down to read a long **pdf** document.

When in Full Screen view you navigate through the document with your mouse or with key strokes. Clicking the left mouse button, or pressing the ⇓ key, opens the next page. Clicking the right mouse button, or the ⇑ key, opens the previous page. The **Home** key moves you to the first page of the document, and the **End** key to the last. To leave Full Screen view you just press the **Esc** key.

Read Mode

 The **Hide Toolbars** button switches on Read mode, which doesn't change your zoom or viewing modes, but gives you more screen area to read pages, by turning off the Toolbars. The menu bar and navigation pane are retained as are a limited selection of tools on the status bar.

 To leave Read mode, you click the **Show Toolbars** button, shown here, which is placed on the status bar in Read mode.

Navigation Controls

These provide a quick way to navigate through documents.

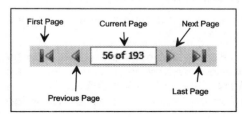

Fig. 2.16 The Navigation Control Buttons on the Status Bar

To jump to a specific page number you can select the current page number in the status bar, type the page number to jump to, and press the **Enter** key.

 There is actually a Navigation toolbar, which we didn't mention previously, which lets you click similar buttons to move forward or backward through your document. To open this Navigation toolbar, right-click in the toolbar area, and then choose **Navigation**.

View Buttons

After you have navigated through a document, you can retrace your path right back to where you started using these two buttons.

    Go back to the **Previous View**.

    Go forward to the **Next View**.

The Next View option is only available if you have chosen a Previous View.

Page Layout Buttons

The four buttons on the right side of the status bar let you control the page layout of the document being read. Changing the page layout is especially useful when you want to zoom out to get an overview of the document layout.

   Single Page displays one page in the document pane at a time. (Fig. 2.17)

   Continuous arranges the pages in a continuous vertical column. (Fig. 2.18)

   Continuous - Facing arranges the pages side by side in a continuous vertical column. If a document has more than two pages, the first page appears on the right to ensure proper display of two-page spreads. (Fig. 2.19)

Facing arranges the pages side by side, displaying only one or two pages at a time. (Fig. 2.20)

The following figures show the results of using these four layout buttons on the same **pdf** document.

Fig. 2.17 Single Page

Fig. 2.18 Continuous

Fig. 2.19 Continuous - Facing

Fig. 2.20 Facing

The Menu System

Each of the seven menu bar options have associated with them a pull-down sub-menu. You can use the mouse or the keyboard to activate the menu. With the mouse, just point to an option on the menu bar and click the left mouse button. This opens the pull-down sub-menu of the highlighted menu option. The sub-menu of the **File** option is shown below.

Fig. 2.21 The File Sub-menu

To select an option on this drop-down menu you drag the mouse pointer down the menu with the left mouse button depressed until the one you want is highlighted (goes blue) and then release the mouse button. If there is a ▸symbol on the right of the option, you must select from a further sub-menu that opens.

Menu options can also be activated directly by pressing the **Alt** key, which underlines one letter in each menu option. You then press the underlined letter on the keyboard to open that menu option. Thus, pressing **Alt** followed by **F**, opens the pull-down **File** sub-menu. You can use the up and down arrow keys to move the highlighted bar up and down a sub-menu, or the right and left arrow keys to move along the options in the menu bar. Pressing the **Enter** key selects the highlighted option or executes the highlighted command.

Pressing the **Esc** key once, closes the pull-down sub-menu, while pressing the **Esc** key for a second time, closes the menu system.

Some of the sub-menu options can be accessed with 'quick key' combinations from the keyboard. With these you press both keys together. Such combinations are shown on the drop-down menus, for example, **Ctrl+P** is the quick key combination for the **Print** option in the **File** sub-menu. See Chapter 5 for a full listing of these keyboard shortcuts If a sub-menu option is not available, at any time, it will display in a grey colour.

The following is a brief description of the standard menu options. For a more detailed description of each sub-menu item, use the **Help** system (to be described shortly).

File   Produces a pull-down menu of mainly file related tasks, such as Opening, Saving and Printing files. You can Email documents to other users, view a specific file's Properties, and finally, you can Exit the program.

Edit   Produces a pull-down menu which allows you to Undo and Redo changes made, Cut, Copy and Paste selected text in some parts of a document, to Select and Deselect all of the contents of a document, to check the spelling of comments added, to Search and Find specific text in a document. You can also set your Preferences and control how Reader operates for you.

View   Produces a pull-down menu which gives you control of how you view and navigate through your documents.

Document   Produces a pull-down menu to help you with the security and accessibility settings of your documents.

Tools   Produces a pull-down menu which gives you access to the toolbar tools.

Window   Produces a menu to let you control the display of existing open windows on the screen, and to swap between them.

Help   Activates the help menu which you can use to access the Adobe Reader built-in Help systems, and to access the Adobe Web site to get online help and support.

Shortcut Menus

Context-sensitive shortcut menus are now one of Windows' most useful features. If you click the right mouse button on any screen feature, or document, a shortcut menu is displayed with the most frequently used commands relating to the type of work you were doing at the time.

The composite screen dump in Fig. 2.22 below shows in turn the shortcut menus that open when selected text, or the Toolbar area is right-clicked. In the first shortcut menu the **Copy To Clipboard** option only becomes effective if you have text selected.

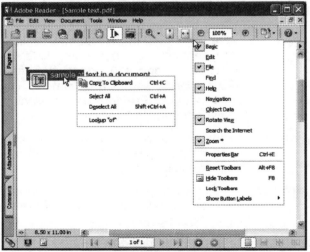

Fig. 2.22 Example Right-click Shortcut Menus

So, whatever you are doing in Adobe Reader, you have rapid access to a menu of relevant functions by right-clicking your mouse. Left-clicking the mouse on an open menu selection will choose that function, while clicking on an area outside the shortcut menu (or pressing the **Esc** key), closes down the shortcut menu.

Dialogue Boxes

If there are three periods (or stops) after a sub-menu option as with the **Open** command in the **Files** menu 📄 Open..., it means that a dialogue box will open when the option or command is selected. A dialogue box is used for the insertion of additional information, such as the name of a file or path.

To see a dialogue box, click the **Open** toolbar button shown here, press **Alt** followed by **F**, and select the **Open** option, or use the **Ctrl+O** shortcut keystrokes. With all of these, the Open dialogue box is displayed, as shown in Fig. 2.23 below.

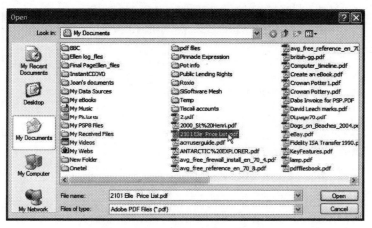

Fig. 2.23 The Open Dialogue Box

When a dialogue box opens, the easiest way to move around it is by clicking with the mouse. Otherwise, the **Tab** key can be used to move the cursor from one column in the box to another (**Shift+Tab** moves the cursor backwards). Alternatively you can move directly to a desired field by holding the **Alt** key down and pressing the underlined letter in the field name.

Within a column of options you can click with the mouse, or use the arrow keys to move from one to another. Having selected an option or typed in information, you must press a command button such as the **Open** or **Cancel** button, or choose from additional options.

Once you have chosen a file to open, to select the **Open** button with the mouse, simply click on it, while with the keyboard you must first press the **Tab** key until the dotted rectangle, or focus, moves to the required button, and then

press the **Enter** key. Pressing **Enter** at any time while a dialogue box is open, will cause the marked items to be selected and the box to be closed.

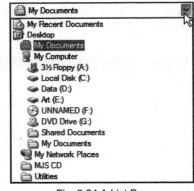

Some dialogue boxes contain List boxes which show a column of available choices, similar to the **Look in** option at the top of the previous screen dump. You open the list by pressing the down-arrow button, as shown here in Fig. 2.24.

Fig. 2.24 A List Box

If there are more choices than can be seen in the area provided, use the scroll bars to reveal them. To select a single item from a List box, either double-click the item, or use the arrow keys to highlight the item and press **Enter**.

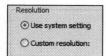

Fig. 2.25 Option
Buttons

Other dialogue boxes contain **Option** buttons with a list of mutually exclusive items, as shown in Fig. 2.25.

The default choice is marked with a green dot against its name, while unavailable options are dimmed.

Other dialogue boxes contain Check boxes, like the ones in Fig. 2.26, which offer a list of options you can switch on or

Fig. 2.26
Check Boxes

off. Selected options show a tick in the box against the option name, while incompatible options appear greyed out. If you want to see examples of all these features, use the **Edit**, **Preferences** command to open the Preferences dialogue box.

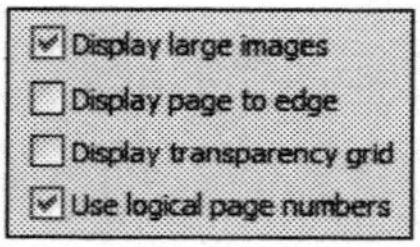

To cancel a dialogue box, either click the **Cancel** button, or press the **Esc** key. Pressing the **Esc** key in succession, closes one dialogue box at a time, and eventually aborts the menu option.

3

Using Adobe Reader

No matter how experienced you are, there will always be times when you need help to find out how to do something in Adobe Reader. It is after all a powerful package with a multitude of features.

Help with Adobe Reader

Adobe Reader 7.0 has no printed user manual, but does have the following built-in Help features:

- The main Reader Help system.
- How To pages, for basic help on common operations.
- Tool tips, which identify the various buttons, tools, and controls in the work area. These appear like this [Help] when you move the pointer over an item.
- Help buttons like this [⬚⬚⬚⬚ Help ⬚⬚⬚⬚] in some dialogue boxes. When you click one, the Help window opens at the relevant page.

The Main Help System

 If you press the **F1** function key, or click the **Help** toolbar button shown here, and select **Adobe Reader Help**, or use the **Help**, **Adobe Reader Help** main menu command, Help will be accessed directly through the Help window.

When activated, the Help system opens in a separate window with two panes, as shown in Fig. 3.1 on the next page. It has a navigation pane on the left and a topic pane on the right. You use the tabs in the navigation pane to find the topics you want to read.

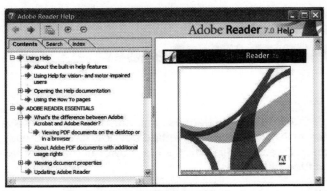

Fig. 3.1 The Adobe Reader Help System

You can drag the vertical bar between the navigation pane and the topic pane to change their widths. When you do this the mouse pointer changes to a ᐳ⫼ᐸ shape. You can also drag the lower right corner to resize the entire Help window.

The Navigation Pane

As shown above, the Help window opens with the **Contents** tab selected in the navigation pane.

The **Contents** tab, (Fig. 3.1) shows the Help topics organised by subject matter. You can click the + or - icons, to the left of the topics, to expand or collapse the list. Clicking a topic name, or the ➡ icon, will open that topic in the topic pane.

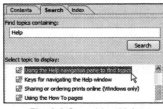

Fig. 3.2 Searching Help

You can click the **Search** tab to find a specific word in Help. You type the word in the text box, as we have done in Fig. 3.2, and click **Search**. The **Select topic to display** list then shows the titles of all topics in which the search word appears. Clicking one of these opens the topic in the topic pane. If you type more than one word, the search results include every topic in which at least one of the words appears.

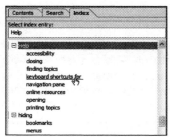

Fig. 3.3 The Index Tab

Clicking the **Index** tab opens an alphabetical list of program features and functions. You can browse the index in two ways.

You can click the + or - controls to expand or collapse the list entries. When you find the term you want, just click a link, as shown here in Fig. 3.3.

Alternatively, you can type an entry into the **Select index entry** text box, as shown above. The list scrolls to the first match of the typed text string. You then click a link to go to that topic, as before.

The Help Toolbar

You can control the Help window with the five buttons on the toolbar, as follows:

 Previous Topic - Steps back to the previous Help topic viewed in the current session list.

 Next Topic - Steps forward to the next Help topic viewed in the current session list. When you close the Help window, you end the Help session and delete its history.

 Print Topic - Prints the current Help documentation topic. Each topic has to be printed individually. It is not possible to print multiple topics at a time or entire Help sections.

 Zoom In - Click this button to zoom the screen magnification of the Topic pane up to the next zoom setting.

 Zoom Out - Click this button to zoom the screen magnification of the Topic pane down to the next zoom setting.

Help on the Internet

The Adobe Reader Help system is quite comprehensive but if all else fails, you can connect to an Adobe Web site with the **Help**, **Online Support** menu command, as shown in Fig. 3.4 below. You must obviously have an Internet connection for this to work, though!

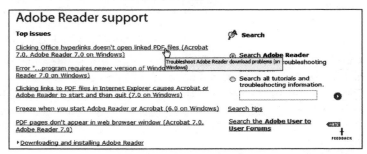

Fig. 3.4 Adobe Reader Online Support

We will leave this for you to explore, but don't forget that the **Help** menu also contains links to various other online resources and references.

The How To Window

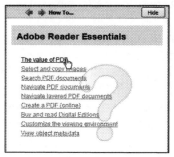

Fig. 3.5 The How To Menu

There are two ways to open the **How To** window shown in Fig. 3.5. Choosing the **Help**, **How To**, **Adobe Reader Essentials** main menu command, or more simply, clicking the **Help** toolbar button and selecting **Adobe Reader Essentials** will both open this pane on the right side of the Reader window. We find this feature of limited use, but you must try it and make your own decisions.

To close the **How To** window click its **Hide** button. You can reposition it by right-clicking its title bar, and choosing either **Docked Left** or **Docked Right** from the context menu. To change the width of the **How To** window, drag the separator bar when the mouse pointer changes to a ◄╫► shape. As with the main Help window, you can use the Back ◄ and Forward ► buttons to navigate among the pages you've viewed in your current session.

Adobe Reader Preferences

Before we go any further, we should look at the way you can set up Adobe Reader to work the way you want. Like most Windows programs, this is done in a Preferences dialogue box, as shown in Fig. 3.6 below. You open this with the **Edit**, **Preferences** main menu command, or the **Ctrl+K** keyboard shortcut.

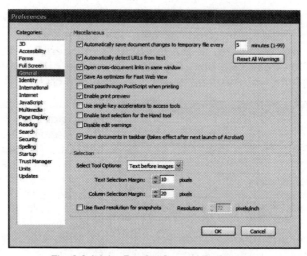

Fig. 3.6 Adobe Reader General Preferences

You select the type of preferences from the **Categories** list on the left. We show the General options above.

On each category sheet select the options you want and when you have finished click the **OK** button. Clicking **Cancel** will leave the settings unchanged.

We don't have the space here to describe all the available settings. Most of them are fairly self-explanatory, but if you need more information try searching the Help system. Don't forget that these preference settings control the way your version of Adobe Reader works not how a specific **pdf** document appears.

Opening a pdf File

Now you have Acrobat Reader installed and set up on your PC it's time to start looking at your **pdf** documents. You can do one of the following to open and view a **pdf** file.

Double-click its icon in a Windows Explorer window to open Adobe Reader with the file already loaded.

 If the Reader is already open, use the **File**, **Open** menu command, or click the **Open** toolbar button shown here, or use the **Ctrl+O** keyboard shortcut. In the Open dialogue box (Fig. 2.2), select the **pdf** document, or documents, you want to work on, and then click on **Open**.

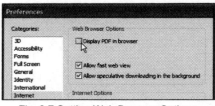

Fig. 3.7 Setting Web Browser Options

The above methods open **pdf** files into a 'free standing' version of Adobe Reader. We saw on page 12 that you can also open a **pdf** file with Reader forming part of your Web browser. This happens by default when you click on a Web site **pdf** link. We prefer to have all **pdf**s opening just in Reader, so have removed the **Display PDF in browser** selection in the Internet section of the **Edit**, **Preferences** dialogue box, as shown in Fig. 3.7 above.

Navigating pdf Documents

The Status Bar Controls

Fig. 3.8 The Navigation Controls

As we saw earlier on page 23 the navigation controls provide a quick way to step through a **pdf** document one page at a time. You can also jump to a specific page number by selecting the current page number in the status bar, (56 of 193 in our example) typing the page number to jump to, and pressing the **Enter** key. This is only of use though, if you know the page number you want to go to. The other methods, described next, use the navigation pane and let you more easily 'jump about' the document you are reading.

Using Navigation Tabs

The navigation pane contains Tabs which display a document's bookmarks, page thumbnails, or 'articles'. Fig. 3.9 shows the Pages tab open and we are dragging the vertical bar between the panes to reduce its width. As usual, the mouse pointer changes to a ⊣⊢ shape to let you do this.

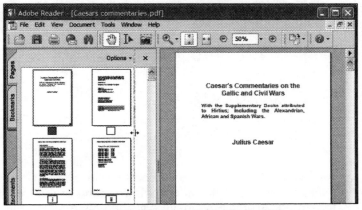

Fig. 3.9 Adjusting the Navigation Pane Width

There are several ways to show or hide the navigation pane. The easiest is to click the tab name on the left side of the document pane. To open and close the currently active tab, move the pointer over the vertical separating bar and click when the pointer changes to the ⊣∣⊢ shape, or simply press the **F4** key. You can also control the tabs from the **View**, **Navigation Tabs** menu.

If you play around with the tabs a little, you will find that you can drag a tab from its location and float it to any location on the screen. If you move it out of the Reader window you can even have several tab sheets open at the same time. Use the **View**, **Navigation Tabs**, **Dock All Tabs** command to return them to their normal positions.

Using Page Thumbnails

As we saw in Fig. 3.9, **Page** thumbnails provide miniature previews of document pages. You can use these thumbnails to change the display in the document pane and to go to other pages in the document. When the **Pages** tab is open you jump to another page by clicking the page's thumbnail.

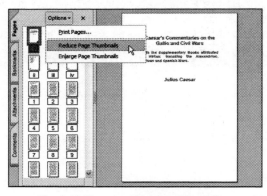

Fig. 3.10 Changing Thumbnail Page Size

As we show above, you can control the size of your thumbnails from the **Options** drop-down menu at the top of the tab. In our example we have considerably reduced their size so that we have more to work with.

To change the display in the document pane from a thumbnail, you can adjust the red page-view box in the thumbnail. This indicates which area of the page appears in the document pane, as shown in Fig 3.11.

Fig. 3.11 Adjusting the Page-view Box

You can resize this box to change the zoom percentage by dragging its right-hand corner when the pointer changes to the ⬉ shape. Fig. 3.11 shows this operation taking place. As you drag the box outline, the view in the document pane zooms up and down.

When the pointer changes to a hand ⟨ᐟ⟩ shape you can drag the red page-view box around the thumbnail. This changes the view in the document pane without changing the zoom percentage.

Fig. 3.12 Changing the Document View

Bookmarks

Bookmarks provide an 'active' table of contents to help document navigation. The creator of the **pdf** document determines what bookmarks if any are used. They usually represent the chapters and sections in a document.

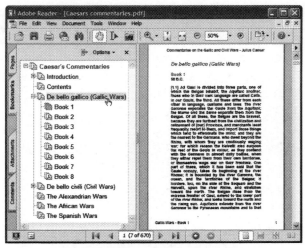

Fig. 3.13 A Document's Bookmark List

You can navigate through a document using its bookmarks. To jump to a topic click its bookmark in the list, as shown in Fig. 3.13 above. This shows another view of the eBook we recently created on Julius Caesar's writings.

You can expand a list by clicking the plus signs (+) next to parent bookmarks. Clicking the minus signs (-) contracts the list. Depending on how the **pdf** document was set up, clicking a bookmark can perform an action as well as, or even instead of, taking you to another location.

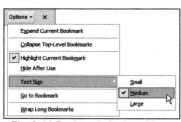

Fig. 3.14 Bookmark Options Menu

If you want the Bookmarks tab to always remain open after you click a bookmark, click the **Options** button at the top of the Bookmarks tab, and make sure that **Hide After Use** is not selected.

Fig. 3.14 shows the other menu options that are available to you to control how bookmarks work for you in your **pdf** document.

Using Links

Clicking a link in a **pdf** document is like clicking a link on a Web page. Links can take you to another location in the current document, to other documents, or even to Web sites on the Internet. The original document creator determines what links look like in a **pdf** document.

To follow a link select the **Hand** tool 🖑, move the pointer over the linked area on the page until the pointer changes to the hand with a pointing finger 🖑. Then click the link to jump to the linked destination. If the link points to a location on the Web the hand pointer has a W next to it, as shown in Fig. 3.15.

Fig. 3.15 An Internet Link

Clicking a link can also open file attachments and, as long as you downloaded the full version of Adobe Reader, can play 3D content, movies, and sound clips.

Articles

Articles are electronic threads created by the **pdf** creator that lead you through a document. An article typically begins on one page and continues on a different page later in the document, in the same way as articles skip pages in traditional newspapers and magazines. When you read an article, the page view zooms in or out so that the current part of the article fills the screen.

To read an article make sure you are not working inside a browser and use the **View**, **Navigation Tabs**, **Articles** command to open the **Articles** tab, as shown here. Then double-click the article's 🔳 icon to start reading the article. If necessary, select the **Hand** tool and then click anywhere in the article to start reading it at that point. When in the article, the pointer changes to 🖑, the follow-article

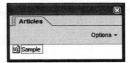

Fig. 3.16 The Articles Tab

pointer. Just keep clicking this to navigate through the article. To go backwards through the document, press the **Shift** key and click in the article, (the pointer then changes to ♨). When you reach the end of the article, the pointer will change to ♨, which is the end-article pointer.

Searching pdf Files

Adobe wants people to use the **pdf** format to store all of their documents, so Acrobat Reader has been provided with several ways for you to find what you are looking for in your **pdf** files. As we shall see, you can search documents to find a part of a word, a word, or a phrase. You can search the document text, comments, bookmarks, and document information. You can search one file or multiple files, and you don't even have to open them all.

Same Document Searches

To search solely in the document that you have open, you can use the **Find** toolbar which has a basic set of search options. If this is not open, use the **Edit**, **Find** menu command, the **Ctrl+F** shortcut, or right-click in the toolbar area and select **Find** to open it.

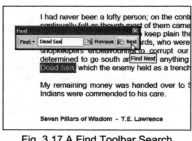

Fig. 3.17 A Find Toolbar Search

In the **Find** text box, type the partial word, word, or phrase, that you want to search for, and click the **Next** button. Reader will very rapidly scroll through the document until it finds the first occurrence of your search text. It will pause with the found text highlighted, as shown in Fig. 3.17. To view each search result in the file, click the **Next** or **Previous** buttons to step forward or backward through the document.

Fig. 3.18 Find Options Menu

Clicking the **Find Options** button ⬚ will open the drop-down menu shown in Fig. 3.18. In this you can match whole words only, make the search case-sensitive, or extend the search to include not only document text but also bookmarks and comments. If you need additional search options, choose **Open Full Reader Search** option to open the **Search PDF** pane covered next.

More Advanced Searches

Clicking the **Search** button, on the File toolbar, opens the **Search PDF** pane shown in Fig. 3.19. This shows the basic search options available which let you search for a word, or phrase, in the current **pdf** document, or in other **pdf** documents on your hard disc, and gives you access to more advanced search options.

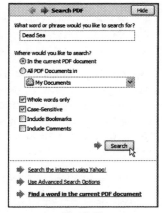

Fig. 3.19
Using Basic Search Options

You type the search text as before, and choose what search options you want by checking the various option buttons and check boxes. When you are ready to start, click the **Search** button. The results appear listed in the pane in page order with a few words of context, as shown in Fig. 3.20 on the next page.

As you move the pointer over the **Results** list a pop-up will show you what page number each search result is on. To display the page that contains a search result just click the item in the list. You will find the text highlighted.

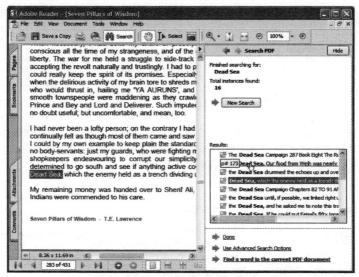

Fig. 3.20 Searching a Large Document

The above search in another of our eBook examples took less than a second, even though there were over 400 pages. Adobe have really produced a very effective tool. To close the Search pane, either click the **Hide** button at the top of the pane, or the **Done** link at the bottom. The document pane then returns to its former size. If you accidentally close the Search PDF pane, simply reopen it and the most recent search results will still be there.

You can search multiple **pdf** files in a folder on your hard disc or on a local network without opening them first. To do this, check the **All PDF Documents in** option button and find the folder by clicking the **Browse for Location** option in the adjacent list box, as shown in Fig. 3.21. The results appear nested under the document names and paths.

Fig. 3.21 Setting a Folder Location to Search

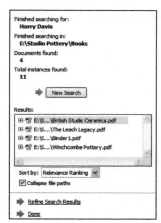

```
Finished searching for:
  Harry Davis
Finished searching in:
  E:\Studio Pottery\Books
Documents found:
  4
Total instances found:
  11

        ⟐ [ New Search ]

Results:
 ⊞ 🖼 E:\S...\British Studio Ceramics.pdf
 ⊞ 🖼 E:\S...\The Leach Legacy.pdf
 ⊞ 🖼 E:\S...\Binder 1.pdf
 ⊞ 🖼 E:\S...\Winchcombe Pottery.pdf

Sort by:  Relevance Ranking ▾
☑ Collapse file paths

 ⟐ Refine Search Results
 ⟐ Done
```

Fig. 3.22 Results of a
Multi-document Search

The results of a typical multiple-document search are shown here in Fig. 3.22.

In the **Results** list you click the plus sign (+) next to a document path and name to expand the results for that document. Clicking a result will open the document in the document pane at the page with the searched-for text highlighted. This type of search can take a little longer, depending on the number and size of **pdf** files to be searched. If you have finished, you click the **Done** link, as before.

Fig. 3.23 shows that you can broaden or restrict your search results by clicking the **Use Advanced Search Options** link at the bottom of the Search PDF pane when it displays the Basic Search options, (as shown in Fig. 3.19).

If you click the **Return results containing** list box, the following extra options are available. Some of these do not apply to a single document search.

```
⟐ ⟐ Search PDF              [ Hide ]

What word or phrase would you like to search for?
[ Crowan                                     ]

Return results containing:
[ Match Exact word or phrase            ▾ ]

Look In:
[ 🗁 E:\Studio Pottery\Books            ▾ ]

Use these additional criteria:
[              ▾ ] [ Is exactly        ▾ ]
□ [                                        ]

☑ Whole words only    ☑ Case-Sensitive
□ Proximity           □ Stemming
□ Include Bookmarks   □ Include Comments
□ Include Attachments

                         ⟐ [ Search ]

⟐ Search the internet using Yahoo!
⟐ Use Basic Search Options
⟐ Find a word in the current PDF document
```

Fig. 3.23
Advanced Search Options

Match Exact Word Or Phrase searches for the entire string of characters, including spaces, in the order in which you type them in.

Match Any Of The Words searches for any instances of at least one of the words typed.

Match All Of The Words searches for instances that contain all your typed search words, but in any order.

The **Boolean Query** option searches for terms or phrases using the following Boolean operators:

Use the **AND** (or **&**) operator between two words to find documents that contain both words.

Use the **NOT** (or **!**) operator before a search term to exclude any documents that contain that term.

Use the **OR** (or **|**) operator between terms to search for all occurrences of either term.

Use **^** (**exclusive OR**) between terms to search for all occurrences that have either operator, but not both.

Use **( )** brackets to specify the order of evaluation of terms in a query. For example the search *pie AND (custard OR coconut)* will retrieve documents that contain the word pie and either of the words custard or coconut.

The Boolean option is not available for single-document searches. Also don't bother to try wildcard searches using asterisks (*) or question marks (?). They do not work.

The options in the **Look In** drop-down list let you restrict the search to the current document, an index, or a location on your computer. If you choose to search an index or a location on your computer the **Use these additional criteria** option appears, as shown in Fig. 3.23. This is described in the next section.

Refining Search Results

After you search more than one document, you can refine your results by adding additional search criteria. With the results of a multi-document search still listed, as shown in Fig. 3.22, click **Refine Search Results** at the bottom of the Search PDF pane. This opens the **Refine Search Results** pane shown in Fig. 3.24 on the next page.

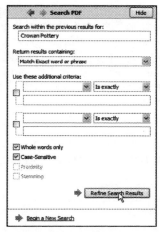

Fig. 3.24 Results of a
Multi-document Search

The **Use these additional criteria** options let you restrict the existing search results to those that match specified date criteria or that contain additional words in a particular document property, such as author, title, subject, file name, keywords, bookmarks, comments, image metadata, XMP metadata, object data, and indexed structure tags.

To do this, select the check box adjacent to a set of search criteria, choose a document property from the first pop-up menu, and then choose a value from the adjacent pop-up menu. In the box below, type the value of the criterion. If you choose date related criteria, you can click the pop-up menu to select the date from an interactive pop-up calendar, as in Fig. 3.25. To add additional document characteristics to the search criteria, use the second set of boxes in the same way. When you are happy with your selections click the **Refine Search Results** button and keep your fingers crossed.

Fig. 3.25 Selecting Date
Criteria

Using an Index

An index is a file, specially prepared in Adobe Acrobat Professional, that catalogues multiple Adobe **pdf** files. If a full-text index is available for a set of documents, you can search the index rather than searching each individual document. This is very much faster.

To search an index, click the **Use Advanced Search Options** link, type the word you want to find and choose the **Select Index** option in the **Look In** box. Select the index you want to use, or click **Add** and locate the index file (.pdx) you want, and then click the **Open** button followed by **OK**, and proceed with your search as usual.

Searching the Internet

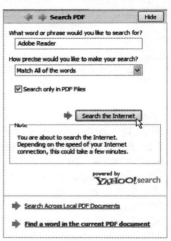

Before we finish with searching, we will mention the **Search the Internet using Yahoo** toolbar button again. This button lets you search for text on the Internet, or in one or more **pdf** documents on your hard disc. It opens the Search PDF pane, as shown here in Fig. 3.26.

The options in this Search pane should by now be self explanatory. If you select the **Search only in PDF files** option, as we have, you will get a listing of the **pdf** files on the Internet that the search engine Yahoo could find that contain your search word, or phrase. If you don't select this, you will get a listing of all the Web pages it could find.

Fig. 3.26
Searching the Internet

We have somewhat laboured this section on searching **pdf** files, but once your documents are stored as **pdf**s, it's obviously important to be able to find things in the future.

In all of the Search PDF panes described, you can retrace your steps by clicking the Back ◀ and Forward ▶ buttons.

Printing pdf Files

Adobe Reader not only lets you read **pdf** files, but usually gives you a good measure of control over printing them, either on paper or over the Internet.

Some Background

When Windows was installed on your computer your printers should have been installed as well. Many hundreds of different printers are supported by Windows so, hopefully, you shouldn't have too much trouble getting yours to work. With Windows XP, the printer and printing functions are included in a single Printers and Faxes folder, which you can open by double-clicking the above icon in the Control Panel window. Our Printers and Faxes folder, shown in Fig. 3.27, has a list of printers available for use, and an **Add a Printer** option under **Printer Tasks**.

Fig. 3.27 The Printers Dialogue Box

This box provides an easy way of adding new printers, configuring existing ones, and managing all your print jobs.

Configuring a Printer

With Windows, all configuration for a printer is now consolidated onto a tabbed property sheet that is accessed from its icon in the Printers and Faxes folder.

Fig. 3.28
Object Menu

Right-clicking a printer icon opens the object menu, shown in Fig. 3.28, which gives control of the printer's operation. If you click the **Properties** option, a dialogue box similar to that in Fig. 3.29 opens and lets you control all the printer's parameters, such as the printer port (or network path), paper and graphics options, built-in fonts, and other device options specific to that printer model.

All these settings are fairly self explanatory and as they depend on your printer type we will let you work them out for yourselves.

Once your printer is set up you should, at any time, be able to use the **File, Print** command from the Reader menu bar, or **Ctrl+P**, to open the Print box, shown in Fig. 3.32 on a later page.

Fig. 3.29 The Printer Properties Box

One very annoying feature of Adobe Reader 7.0 was that however you set your default printer, or program, preferences it always assumed you wanted to print on 'letter size' paper when it first started up. You had to use the **File, Print Setup** command to set the general printing options you wanted, before starting a print process. This problem was resolved in the updated version 7.0.1, so if necessary you should update Reader.

In this box you select the print settings you want, including **Paper, Orientation** and printer **Properties**. You only need to do this once in a working session. Once done, every time

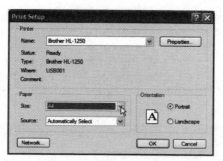

Fig. 3.30 The Adobe Reader Print Setup Box

you print in that session, it will be quite happy to default to A4 paper and the other settings you made.

Printing a pdf Document

When printing whole pages we find it best to set the pages to print by selecting their thumbnails in the Pages tab as shown in Fig. 3.31 below.

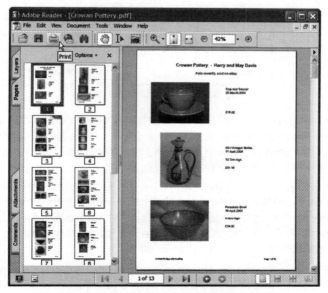

Fig. 3.31 Selecting the Page to Print in the Pages Tab

The usual Windows selection principles apply. To select non-contiguous pages, hold the **Ctrl** key down and click the thumbnails you want. For a contiguous range, click the first and last thumbnails with the **Shift** key depressed. Then click the **Print** toolbar button, choose **File**, **Print** command from the Reader menu bar, or **Ctrl+P**, to open the Print box, shown in Fig. 3.32 below.

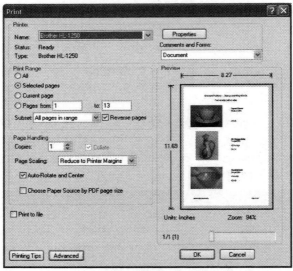

Fig. 3.32 The Print Dialogue Box

This is a very powerful set of print controls. If necessary, you have another chance to choose a printer from the drop-down list in the **Name** list box, or click the **Properties** button to set new printer driver options.

You can also set the pages you want to print in the **Print Range** section, but to get the correct image in the **Preview** pane we find it is better to preselect the pages as previously described. The image in the **preview** pane shows what will be printed with the current selections.

For more detail on any of the printing features we suggest you open the **Printing Adobe PDF Documents** page in the Help system. This is shown in Fig. 3.33.

Fig. 3.33 Getting Help with the Print Settings

 This is a very long Help page and it might be a good idea to click the Print Topic button, shown here, and print it out for future reference.

Printing Over the Internet

You can also print a **pdf** document to a device over the Internet using the **File**, **PrintMe Internet Printing** menu option. As long as you are connected, this opens a Web page which lets you print at public PrintMe printers at "hotels, airports, business centres and fax machines across the globe". Apparently with "no cables, no configuration, and no hassles".

When we tried it out for the UK, we were offered the choice of using printers in three London Hotels and at an office in Bournemouth. Not a lot of use if you are travelling anywhere else in the country, but you might find it useful. At the moment we will put this down as something for the future!

Copying Data from pdf Files

As long as no restrictions have been built into a **pdf** document by its author, you can copy its contents to the Windows clipboard. This lets you use the material in other ways, by pasting it into a word processor or graphics package. There are limitations here though. In Reader you have to copy text and graphics separately. There is a way of copying them together, but the result is a bitmap image and you can't manipulate the text in it.

Copying Text

As usual with Windows, before you can copy text you must first select it. With Reader you use the Select tool, and what you select depends on the page layout that is active. To select text on the current page only, you must set Single Page layout. (See page 24). To select multiple pages of text you use one of the Continuous layouts.

 To select text, click the **Select** tool button, click the I pointer at the beginning of the text to be selected, and with the left mouse button depressed, drag to the end of the required text. The selection area turns black while active and the mouse button is depressed. When you release the button the selection

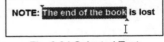

Fig. 3.34 Selected Text

colour changes to blue as in Fig. 3.34. Note the pointers showing the beginning and end of the selection.

If you move the Select tool pointer around a **pdf** page, you will find it changes shape depending on what it is over. When over text you get the I beam pointer as above. Over an image, it changes to a cross hair -¦- pointer. When over empty space adjacent to text it changes to the Column-select pointer. As its name suggests, you can use this pointer to select columns, or rectangles, of text as shown in Fig. 3.35. Any words within or intersected by

Fig. 3.35 Using the
Column-select Pointer

the selection rectangle are selected. You can force this pointer shape anywhere in text by depressing the **Ctrl+Alt** keys.

Double-clicking in a word will select the word. Triple-clicking will select the line of text, and clicking four times will select all the text in a page or the document, depending on the page layout setting (Single Page layout or Continuous layouts respectively). This latter option can sometimes be a little temperamental! Alternative methods are the **Ctrl+A** keyboard shortcut, or the **Edit, Select All** command.

To extend a selection letter by letter, you press **Shift** and an arrow key. To extend a selection word by word, you press **Shift+Ctrl** and the left or right arrow keys. To extend a selection line by line, you press **Shift+Ctrl** and the up or down arrow keys.

To copy the selected text hold the pointer over the selection until a menu appears, and then choose **Copy to Clipboard**, which in our example here is the only option.

Fig. 3.36
Copying Text

You can also use the **Edit, Copy** command to copy the selected text to the clipboard, or right-click in the selection and choose **Copy to Clipboard** from the context menu.

Copying Graphics

Using the Select tool you can copy and paste individual images from a **pdf** document to the Clipboard, and then paste them into another Windows application. When the pointer changes to the cross hair -¦-, it is in image selection mode.

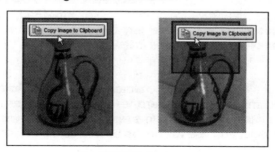

Fig. 3.37 Copying Images
Left - Whole Image Selected   Right - Part of Image Selected

To select the whole image, just click it. To select part of the image, drag a box around the part you want and release the mouse button. If you want to start again simply click outside the selection to deselect it. To copy the selected image hold the pointer over the selection and choose **Copy to Clipboard** as shown in Fig. 3.37 on the previous page.

The Snapshot Tool

 The Snapshot tool makes it very easy to copy an area of a page to the Clipboard. It doesn't matter whether the area contains text, an image, or both, the tool sends a graphic image to the Clipboard.

Fig. 3.38 The
Snapshot Tool

To use it, select the Snapshot tool, and simply drag the cross hair pointer around the area you want, as shown in Fig. 3.38. When you release the mouse button, the selected area is copied straight to the Clipboard, ready for you to paste into another program.

Saving as a Text File

When you want to copy all the text in a **pdf** document, you can also use the **File**, **Save As Text** command instead of selecting it. This will open a new text file (**.txt**) in the location you specify containing all the document text. You will need to open this file in a text editor like WordPad, or in a word-processor, and delete any headers, footers, captions, and footnotes, as all the text is saved.

As we shall see in a later chapter, it is possible to create a **pdf** document by scanning the original pages as graphic images. If this is done at a low resolution the text will be part of the image, and you will not be able to select it as text.

4

More on Adobe Reader

Using Forms

We all know what a 'form' is. If you apply for something formally, you usually have a form to fill in. An application form for a job, for instance. A **pdf** form is a **pdf** document with spaces for you to enter information, called fields. A **pdf** form can contain static or interactive fields. When they are static you can't fill out the form on your computer, it must first be printed, filled in by hand and then mailed to its destination. Interactive form fields, on the other hand, let you fill in the form in Adobe Reader or Acrobat. By clicking a button on the form the data is then sent over the Internet, either attached to an e-mail message or directly to an on-line database.

If you are using Adobe Acrobat you can save your entered form data when you save the **pdf** form. If you are using Adobe Reader you can only save a blank copy of a **pdf** form, unless the author of the form has added special usage rights.

A **pdf** form can contain the following Windows objects; text fields, buttons, radio buttons, check boxes, combo and list boxes. They also often have a Document Message Bar along the top, as shown in Fig. 4.1 below.

Fig. 4.1 A Typical Form Document Message Bar

To make a document's form fields easier to see you can display them with a light blue background by selecting the **Highlight fields** check box in this message bar. If there is a **Highlight required fields** option you can display a red outline around all compulsory fields.

Completing pdf Forms

One form that many of us battle with every year is an income tax return, so perhaps looking at an interactive **pdf** version of this might be of interest! We found one available free on-line, from the following site:

http://www.freefile.co.uk/

We downloaded the 2004 form and opened it in Adobe Reader. The first page is shown below.

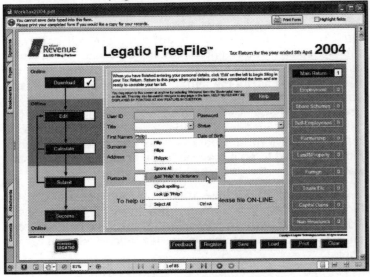

Fig. 4.2 A Very Sophisticated **pdf** Form

At 85 pages this was the biggest form we have encountered so far! No need to panic though, we only use it as an example and if you want to see it for yourself, you now have to pay for the privilege.

To fill in a **pdf** form you work with the **Hand** tool, which as you know by now uses the hand ☜ pointer. When you move the hand tool pointer over an interactive form field, the pointer changes to either a pointing hand ☜, a pointing hand with a plus ☜, an arrow ☝, or an I-beam icon I, depending on the type of field. The I pointer is active when you need to type text, the ▷ pointer lets you select an item in a list box, and the 🖑 and 🖑 pointers let you select a button, a check box, a radio button, or an item from a list. If the form fields are not interactive, the hand pointer does not change.

When you have finished entering text or making a selection in a field, press the **Tab** key to move to the next field, or **Shift+Tab** to return to the previous field. You can press **Esc** to cancel any changes you have made to a field.

When the form is complete click the submit form button, if there is one, to send your entered data to a database somewhere in the world.

Checking Text Spelling

As you enter text into a field any unrecognised words appear with a wavy red underline, as shown in Fig. 4.3. If you right-click in an unrecognised word you can select an alternative from the context menu, or you can open the **Check Spelling** dialogue box. You can only check the spelling of your entered text, not the spelling of text in the underlying **pdf** document.

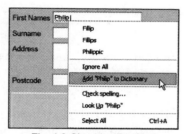

Fig. 4.3 Checking Spelling from the Context Menu

 Another way to check on your spelling, is to wait until you have finished entering text into the form, and then click the **Spell Check** button on the Edit toolbar. This also opens the Check Spelling box, as shown here.

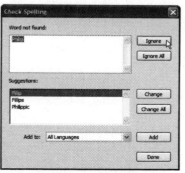

Fig. 4.4 The Check Spelling Box

Completing Fields Automatically

The first time you enter data in a field the message box of Fig. 4.5 opens. This lets you turn on the Auto-Complete feature designed to save time when filling in forms. If the first few characters you type in a form field match something you've typed in a previous form field, the Auto-Complete feature either displays a list of the most probable matches or automatically enters a very probable match for you.

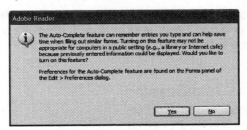

Fig. 4.5 Auto-Complete Message Box

Needless to say, you wouldn't use this if your PC is sited in a crowded office.

Closing a Form

When you have finished working with a form you will probably want to save it. Unfortunately with Reader you can only save the form, not the data you have entered, unless the form itself includes some fancy programming. To save the form, use the **File**, **Save a Copy** command, or **Shift+Ctrl+S**, or click the **Save a Copy** toolbar button. All of these open the following message box.

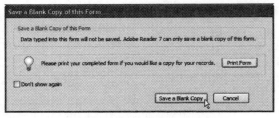

Fig. 4.6 Saving a Blank Copy of a Form

Clicking the **Save a Blank Copy** button, pointed to in Fig. 4.6, will let you do just that, after giving you the chance to change its name.

To close the form you use either the **File, Close** menu command, or the **Ctrl+W** shortcut keys. Before it closes you get yet another message box, like that in Fig. 4.7 below.

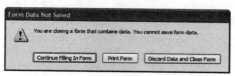

Fig. 4.7 A Final Message Box

This gives you the chance to abort the closure, to print the form with its data as a record, or to actually close the form.

That should be enough about forms to let you handle them with confidence. Don't forget though that there are many companies specialising in just building **pdf** forms. They can include all manner of javascript type programming, so you may encounter many different 'non standard' features.

Picture Tasks

Picture Tasks are included in a 'plug-in' which adds to Acrobat Reader and gives a set of commands which are available in Reader when a Picture Tasks-enabled **pdf** file is opened. Such a file will have been created in an Adobe package, such as Photoshop Album, Photoshop Elements 2.0, or Acrobat.

 Picture Tasks lets you extract **.jpg** images from a Picture Tasks-enabled **pdf** file and save them to your computer. You can also print them locally using standard photo-print sizes and layouts, or send them to an online service provider and have prints mailed back to you.

Installing Picture Tasks

If you have the full version of Adobe Reader (see page 10) the Picture Tasks plug-in will already be installed. If you only downloaded the basic version, when you try for the first time to open a Picture Tasks-enabled **pdf** file you will be asked to install the plug-in. You can download and install just the Picture Tasks plug-in, or have it packaged with two other Adobe plug-ins. The Image Viewer plug-in which lets you view **pdf** multimedia slideshows and eCards, and the Multimedia plug-in, which lets you play sounds and movies. If you prefer, you can install these plug-ins at any time with the **Help**, **Check for updates now** command. Select Multimedia Package from the Current Updates list, click the **Add** button, and then **Update**. If you have time you could also install any other useful updates that are listed.

The How To Window

 The **Picture Tasks** button is activated on the Reader toolbar whenever you open a Picture Tasks-enabled **pdf** file. If the button is not on the toolbar, the open file is not 'enabled' and you will be unable to use these features.

Clicking the button opens a drop-down menu, and you can select a task from this. We find that the easiest way to use the Picture Tasks features, though, is from its page in the How To window opened with the **Help**, **How to**, **Picture Tasks** command. This is shown in Fig. 4.8 below.

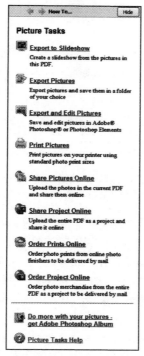

Fig. 4.8 The Picture Tasks How To Window

As shown, this lists all the tasks you can carry out and gives a brief description of each of them. To start a task you just click its underlined link in the list.

You really must try these tasks, they produce some very professional looking results. As an example we will look at the **Export to Slideshow** task, which opens a typical action dialogue box shown in Fig. 4.9 on the next page. We leave it to you to explore the other Picture Tasks. Have fun.

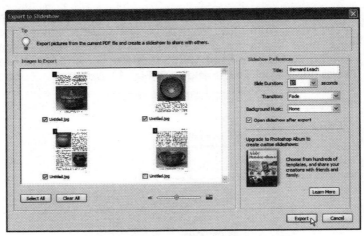

Fig. 4.9 Exporting Image Files to a Slideshow File

In this Export To Slideshow dialogue box, select the images you want to include in the slideshow by clicking in the check boxes alongside each, or by clicking the **Select All** button to include all images. Type in a title and select the **Slideshow Preferences** you want to use, where:

Slide Duration is the time each slide is shown. The options are 1, 2, 3, 4, 5, 10 and 30 seconds.

Transition is the linking effect between slides, such as fade, dissolve, wipe out, etc.

Background Music lets you choose an **.mp3** or **.wav** file from your hard disc to play during the slideshow. This could be a recorded commentary, and is saved with the slideshow file.

When you are ready click the **Export** button pointed to above, select a location and name the slideshow file, then finally click **Save**. If you have left the **Open slideshow after export** box ticked, as in our example above, the slideshow will start and run as soon as it is saved. You now have a **pdf** file that whenever opened will play your slideshow. Ideal for sending to Aunt Gertrude in Australia!

Multimedia Content

As long as you have the full version of Adobe Reader, or have the Multimedia plug-in installed (see page 64), you can play movies and sound clips that have been added to a **pdf** document. You obviously must have suitable hardware and software installed on your PC for playing movies and music. Acrobat Professional is required to add movies and sounds to a **pdf** document.

To play a media clip, make sure your speakers, etc., are turned on, and click the link, bookmark, media clip poster, or the **Play** button if the media clip includes player controls.

Setting Preferences

You can select what media player Reader will use to play movies and sound clips, and set subtitles, dubbed audio, or supplemental text captions. To do this, use the **Edit**, **Preferences** command and select **Multimedia** from the dialogue box shown in Fig. 4.10 below.

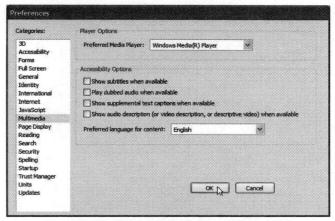

Fig. 4.10 The Multimedia Preferences Dialogue Box

Make sure that you set the correct **Preferred language for content** in case multiple languages are available. Clicking the **OK** button will make the settings active.

Reading Out Loud

Adobe Reader can actually read your pdf documents out loud for you. The electronic voice does sound very much a Dalek though. Exterminate! This feature not only reads a document's main text, but also the text in comment pop-ups and in form fields. It uses the available voices installed on your system. We found four on our system, but we have no idea where they came from!

To read a document out loud, open the page you want to start reading, make sure your speakers are switched on, and use the **View**, **Read Out Loud** command, followed by either **Read This Page Only**, or **Read To End Of Document**.

To force a break at any time, use the **View**, **Read Out Loud**, **Pause**, (**Shift+Ctrl+C**), or the **View**, **Read Out Loud**, **Stop**, (**Shift+Ctrl+E**).

You can control the reading process from its preferences sheet with the **Edit**, **Preferences** command, or **Ctrl+K**, and select **Reading** from the dialogue box shown in Fig. 4.11 below.

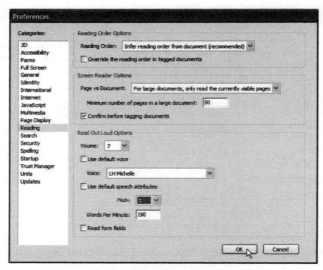

Fig. 4.11 The Reading Preferences Dialogue Box

Adding Comments to pdf Documents

In Adobe Reader 7.0, you can add comments to a **pdf** document as long as it contains 'additional usage rights'. These rights have to be added by the author using Acrobat 7.0 Professional, otherwise the Comment & Markup tools are not available to the document. A message bar similar to that in Fig. 4.12 may show what additional rights the current document has, unless, of course, you have previously opted to not show this type of message.

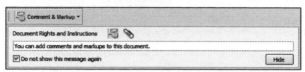

Fig. 4.12 The 'Commenting' Document Message Bar

You might want to add comments to documents for your own use, or as part of a document review procedure. The originator of a document might send it to peers for their comments. Co-authors like us, might send book chapters to each other, for ideas and comments. It can be a useful tool.

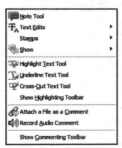

Fig. 4.13 The Commenting Menu

A comment can be a note, the equivalent of a sticky note on paper, highlighting, stamps, and other markup added to a **pdf** document using the commenting tools shown here.

The tools you use to create comments are located on the Commenting toolbar, opened by clicking the **Comments and Markup** button, shown in Fig 4.12 above. You can also access them from the **Tools**, **Commenting** sub-menu shown here in Fig. 4.13.

You can paste copied text and images from the Clipboard into a **pdf** document, or attach a separate file or audio clip. You can also change the way your comments look, both before and after you add them.

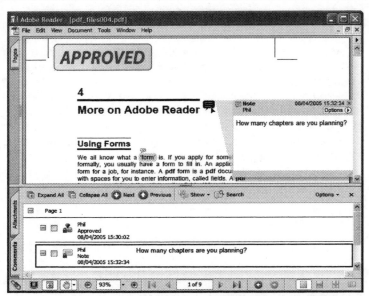

Fig. 4.14 Some Document Comments and the Comments Pane

Our simplistic example above shows several types of comments open in a document. The Comments pane, shown open at the bottom, is a quick and easy way to move between the comments and in some cases to act on the suggestions. All of these comments were made using the Commenting Toolbar shown open here in Fig. 4.15.

Fig. 4.15 The Commenting Toolbar

If you want to go further with using Comments in your **pdf** documents, we suggest you work your way through the extensive listing in the How To pane, opened with the **Help**, **How To**, **Comment & Markup** menu command, and shown on the next page in Fig. 4.16.

Each link opens a pane of explicit and succinct help on how to use and carry out one of the Commenting features. As usual, you click the **Hide** button to close the pane.

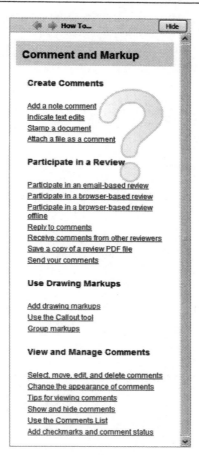

Fig. 4.16 The Comment and Markup How To Window

There is also the Reader Help system. This has a fairly extensive section if you look under Using Commenting Tools in the **Contents** tab.

One thing to remember, though, is that unless a document was given permission by its author when it was created in Acrobat Professional, the **Comments and Markup** facilities will not be available to you when you open it in Adobe Reader.

5

Adobe Reader Shortcuts

A keyboard shortcut is a function key, such as **F5**, or a key combination, such as **Ctrl+A**, that you use to carry out a menu command, or open a tool. An access key, on the other hand, is a key combination, such as **Alt+F**, that moves the focus to a menu, command, or control.

When we first started using computers, graphic interfaces like Windows and pointing tools like mice, had not been invented. The keyboard had to be used for everything, for entering data as well as the commands to manipulate it. Like most people in those days we became quite proficient with the keyboard.

However, times have changed. As Windows has improved as an operating system, pretty well all modern software is designed to be used graphically. You can now spend over half your time using a mouse to move you around a document and to find your way through menus and deep layers of dialogue boxes.

But if you watch a 'professional typist' he, or she, will still use the keyboard for most of the time. The majority of the programs regularly used today are built with a range of keyboard shortcuts. Touch typists find it much easier to learn and use these instead of taking their hands off the keyboard to pick up and play with a mouse.

In this chapter we explain the many keyboard shortcuts built into Adobe Reader 7; many require you to press two keys. For example, **Ctrl+A** means hold down the **Ctrl** key and press the letter **A**.

Menu Command Shortcuts

Many of Adobe Reader 7's keyboard shortcuts are listed on the program's main sub-menus, as follows.

File Menu

Ctrl+O	Open a **pdf** file.
Ctrl+W	Close the current file.
Shift+Ctrl+S	Save a copy of the current file.
Ctrl+D	Open the Document Properties box.
Ctrl+P	Open the Print dialogue box.
Shift+Ctrl+P	Set up the printer.
Shift+Ctrl+9	Print via PrintMe Internet Printing.
Ctrl+Q	Exit the program.

Edit Menu

Ctrl+X	Cut selection to the clipboard.
Ctrl+C	Copy selection to the clipboard.
Ctrl+V	Paste clipboard contents.
Ctrl+Z	Undo the last command.
Shift+Ctrl+Z	Redo the last command.
Ctrl+A	Select all of the current page or of the current document.
Shift+Ctrl+A	De-select all.
Ctrl+F	Find text in the current document.
Shift+Ctrl+F	Start a search operation.
Ctrl+]	Search next document.
Ctrl+[	Search previous document.
Ctrl+G	Next search result.
Shift+Ctrl+G	Previous search result.
Ctrl+K	Open the Preferences dialogue box.

View Menu

F4	Open or close the Navigation pane.
Ctrl+E	Open or close the Properties toolbar.
F8	Hide the toolbars.
Alt+F8	Reset the toolbars.
Ctrl+F8	Dock all toolbars.
F9	Display or hide the main menu bar.
Ctrl+L	View document full screen.
Ctrl+M	Open the Zoom To dialogue box.
Ctrl+1	Zoom to actual size.
Ctrl+0	Zoom to fit whole page in window.
Ctrl+2	Zoom to fit page width in window.
Ctrl+3	Zoom to fit margin width within window.
Ctrl+4	Reflow text.
Shift+Ctrl+H	Start or stop automatic scrolling of text.
Shift+Ctrl+V	Read current page out loud.
Shift+Ctrl+B	Read the rest of the document out loud.
Shift+Ctrl+C	Pause reading document out loud.
Shift+Ctrl+E	Stop reading out loud.
Home	Go to document first page.
⇐	Go to previous page.
⇒	Go to next page.
End	Go to last page.
Shift+Ctrl+N	Go to a specific page number.
Alt+ ⇐	Go back to previous view.
Alt+ ⇒	Go to next view.
Alt+Shift+ ⇐	Go to previous document.
Alt+Shift+ ⇒	Go to next document.
Shift+Ctrl+Plus	Rotate view clockwise.
Shift+Ctrl+Minus	Rotate view anti-clockwise.

Document Menu

Shift+Ctrl+5	Change Accessibility reading options.
Shift+Ctrl+6	Carry out an Accessibility quick check.
Shift+Ctrl+Y	Use local fonts.

Window Menu

Shift+Ctrl+J	Show open windows in cascade view.
Shift+Ctrl+K	Tile open windows horizontally.
Shift+Ctrl+L	Tile open windows vertically.
Shift+Ctrl+W	Close all open documents or windows.
Ctrl+L	Show document in Full Screen view.

Main Keyboard Shortcuts

Before you can use the following shortcuts, you must use the **Ctrl+K** shortcut to open the Preferences dialogue box, click the **General** link, select the **Use single-key accelerators to access tools** option and then press **OK**.

Shortcuts for Selecting Tools

H	**Hand** tool.
Spacebar	Temporarily select **Hand** tool.
V	Current selection tool.
G	**Snapshot** tool.
Shift+Z	Cycle through zoom tools: **Zoom In**, **Zoom Out** and **Dynamic Zoom**.
Z	Current zoom tool.
Ctrl+Space	Temporarily select **Zoom In** tool.
Shift	Temporarily select **Dynamic Zoom** tool (when **Zoom In** or **Zoom Out** is being used).

Moving in a Document

Page Up	Move to previous screen.
Page Down	Next screen.
Home	First page.
End	Last page.
⇐	Previous page.
⇒	Next page.
Alt+ ⇐	Previous view.
Alt+ ⇒	Next view.
Alt+Shift+ ⇐	Previous document.
Alt+Shift+ ⇒	Next document.
⇑	Scroll up.
⇓	Scroll down.
Space	Scroll (when Hand tool is selected).
Ctrl+=	Zoom in.
Ctrl+hyphen	Zoom out.
Ctrl+Space	Zoom in temporarily.
Ctrl+Shift+Space	Zoom out temporarily.
Ctrl+M	Zoom to

Working with Comments

S	**Note** tool.
K	**Stamp** tool.
U	Current highlighting tool.
Shift+U	Cycle through highlighting tools: **Highlighter**, **Cross-Out Text** and **Underline Text**.
J	**Attach File** tool.
Tab	Move focus to comment.
F2	Move focus to text in comment.
Shift+Tab	Move focus to next comment.
Space	Open pop-up window for the comment that has the focus.

General Navigation

F9	Show/hide menu bar.
F10	Move focus to menus.
Shift+F8	Move focus to toolbar in browser or the Help window.
Ctrl+E	Open Properties toolbar, or Properties dialogue box.
Ctrl+F6	Cycle forwards through open documents (when focus is on document pane).
Ctrl+Shift+F6	Cycle backwards through open documents (when focus is on document pane).
Ctrl+F4	Close current document.
F5	Move focus to document pane.
Shift+F5	Move focus from document pane to status bar.
F6	Move focus to next pane or panel.
Shift+F6	Move focus to previous pane or panel.
Space or Enter	Activate selected tool, item (such as a movie or bookmark), or command.
Shift+F10	Open context menu.
F10	Close context menu.
Esc	Close an open menu, or context menu, return to Hand tool and move the focus back to the document pane.
Shift+Ctrl+W	Close all open windows.
Ctrl+Tab	Move focus to next tab in a tabbed dialogue box.
F3	Move to next search result and highlight it in the document.
Shift+arrow keys	Select text (when **Select Text** tool is active).
Shift+Ctrl+ ⇒/⇐	Select previous/next word (when **Select Text** tool is active).
Ctrl+ ⇒/⇐	Move cursor to next/previous word (when **Select Text** tool is active).

Working with Navigation Tabs

F4	Open/close navigation pane.
Shift+Ctrl+F5	Open and move focus to navigation pane.
F6	Move focus between the areas of the document (Document Message bar, navigation panes, and How To window).
Tab	Move focus to next element of the active navigation tab (Options menu, Close box, tab contents, and tab).
⇧ or ⇩	Move to next navigation tab and make it active (when focus is on the tab).
Ctrl+Tab	Move to next navigation tab and make it active (when focus is in the navigation pane).
⇒ or Shift+plus	Expand the current bookmark (when focus is on the Bookmarks tab).
⇐ or minus	Collapse the current bookmark (when focus is on the Bookmarks tab).
Shift+*	Expand all bookmarks.
/	Collapse selected bookmark.
⇩	Move focus to next item in navigation tab.
⇧	Move focus to previous item in a navigation tab.

The Help Window

F1	Open/close Help window.
Alt+F4	Close the Help window.
Shift+F8	Move focus to toolbar in Help window.
⇒ or ⇐	Move focus among tabs: Contents, Search, Index.
Tab	Toggle focus between active tab and tab contents.
⇧ or ⇩	Move to next element in active tab.

The How To Pane

Shift+F4	Open/close the How To pane.
Shift+F1	Open and move focus to How To pane.
Esc	Close the How To pane.
Home	Go to How To home page.
Tab	Move focus down through the elements of the How To pane.
Shift+Tab	Move focus up through the elements of the How To pane.
Ctrl+Tab	Move focus among the elements of the How To pane and the header.
⇨	Go to next page in How To pane.
⇦	Go to previous page in How To pane.

Shortcut Keys for Editing

Ctrl+A	Select all content.
Ctrl+Shift+A	Deselect all content.
Ctrl+9	Browse for a folder.
Ctrl+0	Fit page.
Shift+F5	Move focus to status tray when focus is in the document pane.

Automatic Scrolling

The automatic scrolling feature, activated with the **View**, **Automatically Scroll** menu command or **Shift+Ctrl+H**, makes it easier to scan through a long document. In this mode you can use the following keyboard shortcuts:

0 to 9, or ⇧/⇩	Change the scrolling speed. With the number keys - 9 is the fastest and 0 is the slowest. We find it easier to use the Up and Down arrow keys.
—	Reverse the direction of the scrolling.
⇦ or ⇨	Jump to the next or previous page.
Esc	Stop automatic scrolling.

6

Creating pdf Files

Most **pdf** files contain both text and graphics and are usually first created in application software such a word processors or desk top publishing packages. These files are then converted to the **pdf** format.

In some specialist programs, such as Adobe InDesign, Adobe PhotoShop, Adobe Illustrator, Macromedia FreeHand and CorelDraw, you can use the **Save As** or **Export** commands to painlessly create **pdf** files, but most programs don't have this facility. If the program you work with doesn't, you need extra software. That needn't be a problem as these days, thanks to a large number of software applications that you can install on your PC as '**pdf** Printer Drivers', documents created in almost any program that can print, can be exported as a **pdf** document, or file.

However, not all **pdf** documents are created equal and if you want yours to be able to use all of the sophisticated navigation, optimisation and security features that are available, you can spend hundreds of pounds installing state of the art software, such as Adobe Acrobat Professional.

To a certain extent, you get what you pay for. If you are creating **pdf** files for a large organisation and money is no object, we suggest you go straight to the top and purchase Acrobat Professional. A cheaper alternative is the Standard version of Acrobat, but its features have been pruned. Another option would be to look at an alternative package such as deskPDF, described later. This also comes in Professional and Standard versions, but with the Professional version costing only about $30.00 to download, it's hardly worth bothering with the cut-down Standard version. More on this later.

In this section we give an overview of some of the software available for creating **pdf** files of your own. As mentioned, some is expensive, some not so expensive, and some is even free of charge.

Using Adobe Acrobat Tools

Adobe has developed the **pdf** file format so it is not surprising that their software provides the definitive way to create **pdf** files. But, as mentioned previously, you pay for the privilege. Once installed on your computer, both versions of Acrobat provide all the following tools for creating **pdf** files. In fact they all use Acrobat Distiller to make the conversions. The Professional version gives you a little more control over the properties of the file that is created.

Acrobat Distiller

Using Adobe Acrobat Distiller itself is probably the most confusing way of creating **pdf** files, but once you have mastered it, you will wonder what the problem was. Distiller converts PostScript files into **pdf** files, so you need to be able to convert your original files into PostScript. This may sound a problem, but we assure you it isn't. All Windows application programs that can print to paper can also print to a PostScript file. In Windows, regardless of your actual paper printer, you can install an enormous range of printer drivers and have them available to use in the Printers and Faxes folder, as described on page 51. You use the **Add a Printer** function, and the secret is to install a PostScript printer and set it to print to file.

This is easy with the **Add Printer Wizard** that opens. On its various pages, make sure you select, **Local printer attached to this computer** and in the **Use the following port** option, select **FILE:(Print to File)** from the drop-down list. Next, select a printer that you know will handle PostScript files, as shown in Fig. 6.1 on the next page. Here the actual printer name gave us a clue!

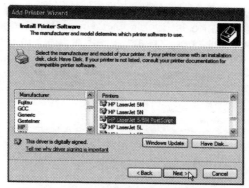

Fig. 6.1 Installing a PostScript Printer Driver

All the driver files for our selection were already on our hard disc as part of the original Windows XP installation, so no further discs were needed.

Once the PostScript printer is added to your list of available printers, you can select to print to it from your application program, and a PostScipt file will be saved wherever you specify on your hard disc. Hopefully your application will have added **.ps** to the end of the file name to indicate it is a PostScript file. If not, you will need to change the name suffix yourself.

Fig. 6.2 The Distiller Splash Screen

From now on, as long as Distiller is set up the way you want, all you have to do is double-click on a PostScript file (.ps) and Distiller will open, create a **pdf** of the same name and save it in the same folder as the .ps file.

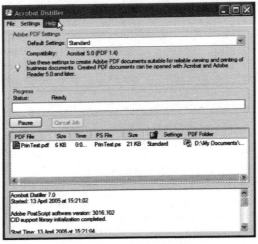

Fig. 6.3 The Acrobat Distiller Window

You can also open Distiller from the Windows **start**, **All Programs** menu system, by selecting **Acrobat Distiller 7.0**. You can then use the **File**, **Open** command to open a PostScript file to convert. This works whatever suffix the PostScript file name has, as long as you select **All Files (*.*)** in the **Files of type** box of the **Open** window.

From the Acrobat Distiller window, shown in Fig. 6.3 above, you can set security for the **pdf** files, choose font locations and watched folders for Distiller, and get **Help** on how to use Distiller. You can also pause, resume, and cancel any active jobs.

With Distiller you can tailor-make **pdf** files depending on how they are going to be used. Your file may need to be to sent to a publishing house, in which case it will need to have best quality graphics and minimum compression. Or it may be for screen use and downloading over the Internet, where quality is less important than file size. You control this in the **Default Settings** box of the Distiller window. Our example in Fig. 6.3 shows **Standard** settings, as suitable for general business use. The other options are, **High Quality Print** for sending to printers, **Press Quality** for high-quality prepress printing, and **Smallest File Size** for screen and Internet use. You can customise these if you ever need to, by selecting the settings that most closely resemble your desired output, modifying them, and then saving them with a unique file name. They will then appear on the available list, as described later on page 149.

Adobe PDF Printer

When Adobe Acrobat is installed on a PC, it adds the Adobe PDF printer to the Printers and Faxes folder. The new icon is shown here. This lets you create **pdf** files from any application that has a **Print** command. So from any application, like your word processor or desk top publisher, when you want to create a **pdf** file of your current document, you use the **File**, **Print** command and select **Adobe PDF** as the printer to use. You can click the **Properties** (or it might be **Preferences**) button to control the printer settings, as shown in Fig. 6.4 below..

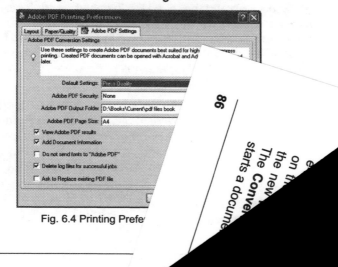

Fig. 6.4 Printing Prefe'

When you finally click the **Print** button, your source document is automatically converted to PostScript and fed directly to Distiller for conversion to **pdf**, without you having to start Distiller. The current Distiller preference settings and **Adobe pdf** printing preferences are used to convert the file. Note that the **Default Settings** box is the same as that described earlier for the Distiller window. You control where the **pdf** file is placed in the **Adobe PDF Output Folder** box, as shown in Fig. 6.4. It is saved with the same name as the source file.

PDFMaker and Microsoft Office

If you use a recent version of Microsoft Office or AutoCAD and have installed Adobe Acrobat 7 on your PC, you should have another easy way to create **pdf** files.

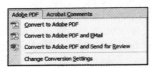

Fig. 6.5 PDFMaker Menu
in Microsoft Word

Fig. 6.6 PDFMaker Toolbar
in Microsoft Word

PDFMaker should have been installed, and toolbars and menus should have been added to Microsoft Word, Access, Excel, and PowerPoint, as shown in Figs. 6.5 and 6.6 above. By default, **pdf** files created using these tools preserve any links, styles, and bookmarks which are present in the source file.

To convert a Microsoft Office file to a **pdf** file, open it in its Office application and either click the **Convert to Adobe PDF** toolbar button, or use the **Adobe PDF, Convert to Adobe PDF** menu command. If you want to send it as an e-mail, click the **Convert to Adobe PDF and EMail** button the toolbar. This opens your default e-mail program with pdf file automatically attached to a new message. **to Adobe PDF and Send for Review** option review process.

The **Adobe PDF**, **Change Conversion Settings** menu command gives you control of the conversion settings, as shown in Fig. 6.7 below.

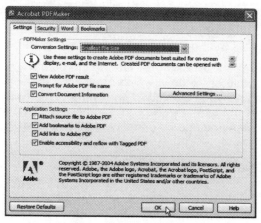

Fig. 6.7 Adobe PDFMaker Control Settings

Most of these settings options are fairly self explanatory and similar to the tools described earlier. The **Advanced Settings** button lets you fine tune the Distiller settings. One thing to remember is that Distiller by default uses the settings that were active the last time it was used. So changes made in Distiller itself and when using the Adobe PDF Printer may affect options in the **Advanced Settings** sheets of the PDFMaker conversion settings.

PDFMaker and Internet Explorer

Fig. 6.8 The PDFMaker Menu

When Acrobat is installed, it adds the **Adobe PDF** toolbar shown here to Internet Explorer. This lets you very easily convert the currently displayed web page to a **pdf** file, or add it to an existing **pdf** file. With both these options you are given the chance to give a filename and location for the new file.

In Windows XP, if you don't see the button in Internet Explorer, use the **View**, **Toolbars**, **Adobe PDF** command.

The **Print Web Page** option can be useful. It converts the current Web page and reformats it to a standard page size with logical page breaks. This can sometimes give much better results than normal printing from a browser window.

The **Adobe PDF Explorer Bar** option opens a pane in the Internet Explorer window, which provides a convenient place for managing your converted web pages. You can rename and delete folders and files in the normal Windows ways. Only **pdf** files and folders containing them are listed.

PDFMaker and Microsoft Outlook

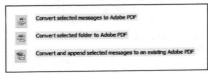

Fig. 6.9 PDFMaker Toolbar Buttons

When Acrobat is installed, it also adds the **PDFMaker 7.0** toolbar, shown here in Fig. 6.9, to Outlook the Office e-mail program.

This lets you convert selected e-mail messages, or a whole folder, to a **pdf** file or append it to an existing **pdf** file. This feature is ideal for archiving your e-mail messages and is well worth trying out.

Using Adobe Acrobat Itself

Fig. 6.10 Acrobat's
Create PDF Menu

There are several ways of creating **pdf** files from the Acrobat program itself. These are accessed from the **Create PDF** toolbar button, shown here, or from the **File**, **Create PDF**, sub-menu, which has the same options. **How To...Create PDF** opens a How To pane in the Acrobat window to give help on all these options.

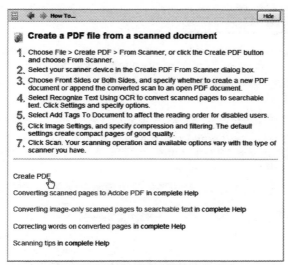

Fig. 6.11 A Typical Acrobat How To Pane

The **From File** option on Acrobat's Create PDF menu (see Fig. 6.10) lets you create a **pdf** from a range of file types, as shown in Fig. 6.12. These are mostly graphic file types which it converts itself. With the others, like Microsoft Office, it opens the application first and then carries out the conversion to **pdf**.

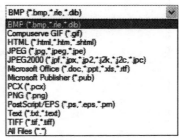

Fig. 6.12 List of Supported File Types

It is so easy to get very clear help, as shown in Fig. 6.11 above, that we will leave it to you to explore these methods of creating **pdf** files.

Online at Adobe

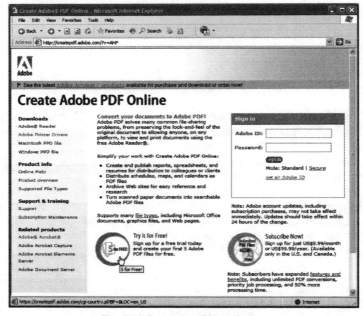
As long as you are online, you can get Adobe to convert your application files to **pdf** over the Internet. When we tried this the URL, or Web address, was as follows:

http://createpdf.adobe.com

At that time, you could get a free trial and convert up to five files, or pay $9.99 a month or $99.99 a year, to make as many **pdf** files as you like.

Fig. 6.13 Creating **pdf** Files Online

You must first register and then upload your supported application file (many formats are supported) or point to a Web page URL and the system does the rest. You choose to either download the finished **pdf**, or have it sent to you as an e-mail attachment. It must be worth a try.

Jaws pdf Creator

Fig. 6.14 Jaws pdf Creator

This is a cheaper commercial equivalent to Acrobat Distiller, created by Global Graphics, and costing around £55.00. According to their Web site, it provides an affordable and reliable means of creating **pdf** files from virtually any document in any application. Using Jaws, you can easily create electronic documents that can be shared across a wide range of hardware and software.

Jaws can be used in several modes. As a printer in the Windows environment, letting you print to a **pdf** file from your application. It also appears as a desktop icon allowing drag-and-drop conversion of any PostScript or EPS file directly to **pdf**. It has three pre-defined settings, Press Ready, Web and Print Quality.

A toolbar icon installs in Microsoft Word, Excel and PowerPoint, allowing you to easily create **pdf** files from these Windows programs. When used this way, bookmarks and hyperlinks from the original document are retained.

If you want to try this package, their Web site is at:

www.jawspdf.com

As with all programs of this type, you will still need to use Adobe Reader for looking at your **pdf** files.

deskPDF

Another cheaper commercial equivalent to the Acrobat Distiller program is deskPDF. This is a simple print driver that produces Adobe Acrobat compatible documents, but you still need to use Adobe Reader to access your **pdf** files. The Professional download version of this package was selling at $29.95 at the time this was written. At that price, it must be worth a try. The Web address was:

www.docudesk.com

We downloaded the Professional version by following the Download links on the site to the following product matrix.

Downloads			
software	**size**	***ftp link**	**http link**
deskPDF Versions			
deskPDF 2.11 Standard	6.9mb	download	site1 site2
deskPDF 2.11 Professional	8.1mb	download	site1 site2
deskPDF 2.11 Standard (zip)	6.9mb	download	download
deskPDF 2.11 Professional (zip)	8.1mb	download	download
deskPDF 2.1 Standard TS Demo	6.9mb	download	site1 site2
deskPDF 2.1 Professional TS Demo	10.2mb	download	site1 site2
deskPDF Documentation			
Standard User Guide (pdf)	633k	download	download
Professional User Guide (pdf)	777kk	download	download

Fig. 6.15 deskPDF Available Downloads

Here we selected one of the **http links** and then downloaded the User Guide in **pdf** format. The file **deskPDF211Pro-Setup.exe** was saved in our default download folder, it was quite large at 8.1MB.

Double-clicking this file in its folder window started the fairly normal Windows installation procedure. We were surprised to be told that a PostScript interpreter had not been found on our system, even though Distiller was present.

No problem though, as it offered to install the Ghostscript interpreter (see page 96). We accepted this option and Docudesk GPL Ghostscript 8.15 was quickly installed. The whole process took less than five minutes.

Using deskPDF

 When deskPDF is installed it adds the deskPDF printer to the Printers and Faxes folder. The new icon is shown here. This lets you create **pdf** files from any application that has a **Print** command. So from any application, like your word processor or desk top publisher, when you want to create a **pdf** file of your current document, use the **File**, **Print** command and select **deskPDF** as the printer to use. Make sure the **Print to file** option is not checked. When you have set your print options and clicked the **Print** button, the save PDF Document dialogue box is opened, as shown in Fig. 6.16 below. This is shown here with **Display Advanced Options** selected..

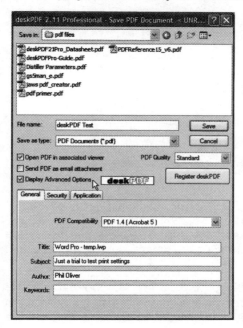

Fig. 6.16 The Save PDF Document Box with Advanced Options

In this box you name the resulting **pdf** file and choose the folder to hold it. If you have Acrobat Reader installed, you will have the option of automatically launching the created document in it.

In the **PDF Quality** drop-down list there are four options to choose from, depending on what the file is to be used for, Web/Email, Printing, Prepress, or the default option, Standard. These are almost the same as Distiller's options described previously on page 85.

When the **Display Advanced Options** box is checked, the dialogue box is expanded to hold the three tabbed sheets of more advanced settings, as shown in Fig. 6.16 on the previous page, and 6.17 and 6.18 below.

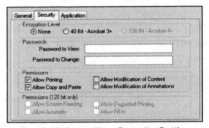

Fig. 6.17 Controlling Security Settings

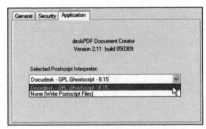

Fig. 6.18 Selecting a PostScript Interpreter to use

The **General** settings sheet (Fig. 6.16) lets you add meta data information about your document, such as its title and author.

The **Security** settings (Fig. 6.17) let you encrypt the document, or give it a password which will be needed to open it in the future. If you want to be able to print the document, or copy text from it, you must check the **Allow printing** and **Allow Copy and Paste** options. Surprisingly, these are not selected by default. To enable changes to be made in the document's comments or annotations, you should select the **Allow Modification of Annotations** option. If you select the **128 Bit Acrobat 4+** encryption level, another four permission options are offered, but not if you have a demo version of the program. These are:

Allow Screen Reading - Allows accessibility programs, such as those for the visually impaired, to convert the **pdf** text into HTML or ASCII so they can be presented in a more legible way.

Allow Assembly - Lets you replace, rotate, insert, and delete pages in the converted **pdf** document.

Allow Degraded Printing - This restricts the printing quality to 150dpi to prevent publication of your document.

Allow Fill-in - Permits users to enter data into form fields.

The **Application** tab sheet (Fig. 6.18) lets you select a PostScript Interpreter to use for the conversion.

When you finally click the **Save** button, your source document is automatically converted to PostScript and fed directly to Ghostscript for conversion to **pdf**. We find that the deskPDF printer works well, and gives good results.

Desktop Drag and Drop

 By default, when deskPDF 2.1 is installed it places an icon on the desktop, as shown here. You can quickly drag and drop documents onto this deskPDF icon to start the **pdf** creation process. The Save PDF Document dialogue box will open for you to control the conversion process, as described previously.

Drag and drop does not work with all of your documents. We could not get it to work with our WordPro word processor files, which seemed a little surprising. All of our Office documents worked fine though.

Right-click Conversion

Another feature added at installation is the deskPDF file conversion option in the right-click menu. To use this, you simply right-click on a supported document's icon in a Windows folder and choose the **Convert with deskPDF** option. Once again this doesn't work with our WordPro word processor files, but does with Office documents.

Other PDF Printer Drivers

There must be hundreds of companies offering packages similar to the ones we have discussed so far. We have not tried any others ourselves, but if you want to search for even better value, we suggest you go to :

http://www.download.com

Just type 'pdf' in the Search box at the top of the screen and work your way through the long list that appears. One that caught our eye was PDF ReDirect 2.0. This was free, but you will have to try it for yourself.

Ghostview and Ghostscript

If you are prepared to spend a little time setting up and getting to know a **pdf** and PostScript system, then have a look at Ghostview and Ghostscript software. As shown in Fig. 6.19 on the facing page, the package is available as a free download complete with instructions from:

http://www.cs.wisc.edu/~ghost/

Ghostscript is the name of a set of software that provides:

- An interpreter for the PostScript language, with the ability to convert PostScript language files to many raster formats, view them on displays, and print them on printers that don't have PostScript capability.

- An interpreter for Portable Document Format (**pdf**) files, with the same abilities.

- The ability to convert PostScript language files to **pdf** (with some limitations) and vice versa.

Put simplistically, it can view PostScript files and save them into **pdf** files. Very rarely, some fonts may not display perfectly on the screen with Acrobat Reader, but they usually print correctly.

 Ghostscript, Ghostview and GSview

Welcome to the Home Page for Ghostscript, an interpreter for the PostScript language and for PDF, and related software and documentation.

Software available at this site

- AFPL Ghostscript current stable release
  - Obtaining AFPL Ghostscript 8.50
- GPL Ghostscript
  - GPL Ghostscript 8.15 released 2004-09-23
  - GNU Ghostscript 7.07 released 2003-05-17
- AFPL Ghostscript developer and beta filesets
- Ghostview and GV previewers for Unix & VMS
- MacGSView previewer for MacOS
- GSview previewer for Windows, OS/2 & Linux.
  - GSview 4.7 released 2005-03-26.
  - GSview can be used as a viewer for Netscape Navigator and Internet Explorer
  - epstool for adding and removing DOS EPS previews
- RedMon - Redirect a Windows printer port to Ghostscript.
  - RedMon 1.7 released 2001-10-28
- ansi2knr - Convert ANSI C programs to traditional ("Kernighan & Richie") C.

Other sites

- FTP mirror sites. Please download from one near you.
- Ghostscript news and community site
- Obtaining GSview and Ghostscript on CD-ROM
- Links to other sites

Documentation

- Frequently Asked Questions
- Introduction to Ghostscript
- Ghostscript documentation
- Ghostscript manual by Thomas Merz
- Gripes
- Printer compatibility
- Newsgroups for Ghostscript
- Books about PostScript

Last updated 2005-03-26. Corrections to the Ghostscript WWW pages should be mailed to Russell Lang

Fig. 6.19 Ghostscript's Home Page

A full English manual in **pdf** format is available for free download from the following location:

ftp://mirror.cs.wisc.edu/pub/mirrors/ghost/gs5man_e.pdf

This should give you enough information to get started with Ghostscript. Good luck if you go this way. You should find it worthwhile in the end.

7

Adobe Acrobat

As we have seen so far, the freely available Adobe Reader is an ideal way both to read **pdf** documents on the screen and to print them. Reader's big brother, Adobe Acrobat, has all of Reader's features, but it can create and manipulate **pdf** documents as well.

In the last chapter we looked at ways of creating **pdf** files and saw that there are many options for 3rd party **pdf** creation software. So although Acrobat is not a requirement for creating **pdf** files, it is the reference standard for creating and managing them. As such we base the rest of this book on Acrobat software and recommend that, if at all possible, you become familiar with the package.

The current version 7.0 was released early in 2005 and comes in two 'flavours', Standard and Professional. Both include a wide range of features, such as the ability:

- To create **pdf** files with pushbutton ease from a wide variety of software.
- To optimise **pdf**s for use online or for printing.
- To change, correct and extract content.
- To add navigational and interactive capabilities.
- To perform document review and comment cycles.
- To perform batch operations on files.
- To rapidly search collections of **pdf** files.

The Standard version costs considerably less than the Professional but it does have the following features missing:

- You can't enable a document so that anyone with the free Adobe Reader software can use the commenting tools, such as the highlighter, sticky note, pen, etc.
- You cannot embed multimedia, sound and 3D graphics in a document.

- You can't create forms in a document.
- It has more limited features when creating from AutoCAD, Microsoft Visio and Microsoft Project.
- There are less features for optimising files for high quality printing.
- You cannot catalogue and build indexes of **pdf** documents.
- There are less accessibility features for impaired users.

As none of these limitations affect the content of this book, we have used the Standard version of Acrobat. This also means the book will still be usable well after newer versions of Acrobat are released.

Installing Acrobat

When we last looked, it was cheaper to order the CD version of Acrobat, than to download it from their Web site. Don't be surprised though if it is mailed from the US, even if you order and pay for it in the UK. This is the age of multinationals.

Before installing Acrobat it is best to restart Windows and turn off any antivirus software. Then either, insert the CD and click **Install Acrobat 7.0** in the Autoplay menu that opens, or if you downloaded Acrobat, double-click the **setup.exe** file.

Follow the instructions in the dialogue boxes that open. When asked, enter your name, organisation if relevant, and the serial number for your copy of the program. This should be on the outside of the CD case, or on an e-mail message page for Web purchases.

Next select the type of installation that you want, where:

- **Typical** installs the program files for Acrobat, Acrobat Distiller, Adobe Designer, PDFMaker, the Adobe PostScript printer driver for your system, standard plug-ins, accessories, and the online documentation.
- **Complete** installs all of Acrobat's features.

- **Custom** lets you specify which components to install.

When the installation is finished, you will be prompted to activate your version of Acrobat. Yes, Adobe have gone the same way as Microsoft and now make you activate their software. If you don't it will stop working after 30 days!

Product Activation

Adobe's activation procedure is designed to deter copying of their software. It is a simple, anonymous process, which in our case happened before we knew anything about it! The program assigns an activation number to your specific computer. When it is activated, this number and your Acrobat serial number are sent to Adobe so they can check that the software is not activated on more than the permitted number of computers. Activation is possible on two machines, as long as Acrobat is not used simultaneously on both of them.

Apparently you can choose to activate either by Internet or phone, but if you are already connected to the Internet, as we were, the activation happens automatically! Activation is not the same as product registration, which is a voluntary process where you provide Adobe with information such as your name, address, e-mail address and product serial number. Apparently registration information is stored separately from that provided to Adobe during activation.

Activation Transfer

Warning - The activation procedure means you have to be very careful when you change your PC or hard disc. You have to 'deactivate' Acrobat while everything is still working. You do this with the **Help**, **Transfer Activation** command while you are connected to the Internet. Once it is deactivated, you will no longer be able to use Acrobat until it is installed and activated on another computer, or back on the original one. If you uninstall Acrobat you will be asked whether you want to transfer the activation.

Looking at Adobe Acrobat

Adobe
Acrobat 7.0

Double-clicking the new Acrobat desktop button shown here, or clicking the **start**, **All Programs**, **Adobe Acrobat 7.0** cascade menu item will open Adobe Acrobat, as shown below in Fig. 7.1.

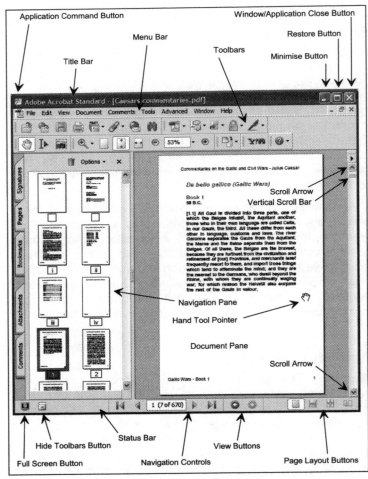

Fig. 7.1 The Adobe Acrobat Screen Layout

The Acrobat Window

The default Acrobat window, or work area, is shown in Fig. 7.1 on the facing page, with a **pdf** file loaded. In fact it is one of the eBooks we have made. If you look back to page 13, you will see that the Acrobat window is almost the same as the Reader window. There is an **Advanced** menu option, a Signature tab in the Navigation pane, and some extra Toolbars. So for a description of the layout and general features of the window, look at the section on Reader starting at page 13 in chapter 2. To make life easier for you, and to save possible confusion, we have included details of the default Acrobat toolbars here, although some of the tools are the same as those in Reader, some are not.

The Toolbars

Fig. 7.2 The Toolbars Menu

There are fourteen different toolbars available in the toolbar area of Adobe Acrobat. To see the full list you can use the **View**, **Toolbars** menu command, or more easily, right-click in the toolbar area. Both methods open the menu shown here in Fig. 7.2. In this list the default active bars are shown with a tick in a blue box to their left. Clicking on a list entry will toggle that toolbar on or off. By default, only seven bars are active, as shown here.

If you hold the mouse pointer over a tool button you will see the name of the tool in a yellow message bar. Holding the pointer over the gripper bar on the left edge of a toolbar will show the name of the toolbar, as shown here for the Zoom toolbar.

Not all the buttons (or icons) are visible at any one time. To see other available buttons click the toolbar options button ✷ at the right end of each bar, as shown in Fig. 7.3.

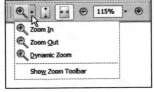

Fig. 7.3
The Zoom Toolbar

As usual with Windows applications, clicking any of the toolbar buttons will action that function. With many, the mouse pointer will change to show what function is active. It will stay active until another is chosen from the toolbars. The **Hand** tool is the default tool.

In the next section we describe the functions of the buttons on the default toolbars.

The File Toolbar

The **File** toolbar contains icons that you click to carry out some of the more common Acrobat 'housekeeping' actions, as follows:

Button   Function

 Open an existing **pdf** file.

 Create PDF from Web Page - Opens a dialogue box for you to enter a Web page URL. The page, or the whole site, is converted to a **pdf** on your PC.

 Save the current document to disc using its existing name. Note that this is different from the Reader's Save As function.

 Print - Opens the Print dialogue box so you can control a printing operation.

 Organizer - Opens the Organizer window in which you can look after and organise the **pdf** files on your computer. Clicking the options button ✷ gives access to the next three buttons.

Add to a Collection - Opens a dialogue box in which you can select to add the current file to any of your Collections. You can also choose to create a new Collection.

 Collections - Gives you rapid access to the collection folders you have created, to group similar **pdf** files together.

 History - Lets you select and open **pdf** files that you have accessed or worked on previously.

 Attach a File - Opens your default e-mail program with the current file as an attachment.

 Attach a File as a Comment - Opens your default e-mail program with the current file as an attachment.

 Email - Opens your default e-mail program with the current file as an attachment.

 Search - Opens the Search PDF pane which lets you search for a word, or phrase, in the current **pdf** document, or in other **pdf** documents on disc.

The Tasks Toolbar

Some of the tools on this bar depend on the contents of the current **pdf** file. The **Picture Tasks** tool, for example, only appears when a Pictures Task enabled file is opened in Acrobat. These extra tools are added to the work area, when they are available.

Button   Function

 Create PDF - Opens a drop-down menu giving the following five ways of creating new **pdf** files, and gives access to the **Create PDF** How To pane .

 From File - Opens a dialogue box for you to choose a file to convert to **pdf**. Supported file types are, text, the more popular types of graphics, HTML and Microsoft Office.

From Multiple Files - Opens a dialogue box for you to choose files to be converted and combined into one **pdf** file. Supported file types are, text, the more popular types of graphics, HTML and Microsoft Office.

 Create PDF from Web Page - Opens a dialogue box for you to enter a Web page URL. The page, or the whole site, is converted to a **pdf** on your PC.

 From Scanner - Opens a dialogue box to control the operation of converting paper documents to a **pdf** file using your scanner. OCR text recognition can be included to make the file searchable.

 From Clipboard Image - Creates a **pdf** file from the current contents of the Windows clipboard.

 Comment & Markup - Opens and closes the Commenting toolbar. Clicking the options button opens a drop-down menu giving control over various commenting and markup operations.

 Send for Review - Opens a menu that lets you send the current document for review by e-mail or in a Web browser, or open a Tracker window which lets you easily manage your reviews.

 Secure - Opens a menu of options that give you control over the security of the current document.

 Sign - Opens a menu that lets you sign the current document. You would usually do this to indicate your approval of the document after all the changes you want have been made.

The Basic Toolbar

This toolbar is the same as that in Reader and is a bar of icons that you click to open basic Adobe Acrobat tools, as follows:

Button   *Function*

Hand Tool - You click and drag this tool to move around a page and view all the areas of it.

Select Tool - Used to select text (I pointer), or an image (÷ pointer) in a **pdf** document. You can then use the Copy and Paste commands to copy the selection to another application, like a word processor.

Snapshot Tool - Used to copy the contents of the selection (text, an image, or both) to the Clipboard or to another application. Both text and images are copied as an image.

The Zoom Toolbar

This contains buttons that you click to give several methods for magnifying the view of **pdf** documents between 1% and 6,400%. With the Zoom Tool buttons, the mouse pointer actually changes to the tool, until another tool is selected.

Button   *Function*

Zoom In Tool - You click this tool on the page to make the text larger. To zoom in on a specific area, use the tool to draw a rectangle. When this tool is selected, you can hold down the **Ctrl** key while clicking or dragging to zoom out instead. Clicking the options button gives access to the next two buttons.

Zoom Out Tool - You click this tool on the page to make the text smaller and view a larger area. When this tool is selected, you can hold down the **Ctrl** key while clicking or dragging to zoom in.

Dynamic Zoom Tool - You click this tool in the text and then drag it, **up the screen** to zoom in to the area where you clicked, or **down** to zoom out. This tool needs playing with, to get used to it.

Actual Size - Used to return the page view to its actual size. This will be 100% unless the document has been set to open at different percentage view.

 Fit Page - Used to resize the page to fit entirely in the document pane.

 Fit Width - Used to resize the page to fit the width of the window or document pane.

 Zoom Out - Click this button to zoom out the screen magnification to the next zoom setting. This does not change the mouse pointer.

 Zoom Menu - Click the down arrow ⊜ to open a drop-down menu of specific zoom options and percentages. If you click the percentage number in the zoom box it will be highlighted, and you can then type in another specific zoom magnification %. Pressing the Enter key will activate it.

 Zoom In - Click this button to zoom in the screen magnification to the next zoom setting. This does not change the mouse pointer.

The Rotate View Toolbar

This toolbar contains two buttons that you can click to change the view of a page in 90-degree increments. These do not change a page's actual orientation, only how you see it in Acrobat.

Button   *Function*

 Rotate Clockwise - You click this button to rotate the current page 90 degrees in a clockwise direction.

 Rotate Counterclockwise - You click this button to rotate the current page 90 degrees in an anti-clockwise direction.

To display both these buttons at the same time in the toolbar, click the options button ▦ and choose **Expand This Button** from the drop-down menu, as shown in Fig. 7.4. To return to the normal button view, click the **Rotate Clockwise** arrow button ▯ to the right of the expanded buttons.

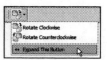

Fig. 7.4
Expanding Bars

The Search the Internet Toolbar

This toolbar contains only one button.

 Search the Internet using Yahoo - This button lets you search for text on the Internet, or in one or more **pdf** documents on your hard disc. It opens the Search PDF pane, as shown here in Fig. 7.5.

The options in this Search pane are all self explanatory, so we will not spend long here. If you select the **Search only in PDF files** option, as we have, you will get a listing of the **pdf** files on the Internet that the search engine Yahoo could find that contain your search word, or

Fig. 7.5 The
Search PDF Pane

phrase. If you don't select this, you will get a listing of all the Web pages it could find. When you click **Search the Internet** your browser will open and the search operation will be carried out from it.

The Help Toolbar

This toolbar contains only one button.

 Help - You click this button to open a drop-down menu of Help options, as shown in Fig. 7.6.

The first group all open a **How to..** Pane to give you quick access to basic help when you start using the program. As long as you are connected to the Internet, **Online Support** opens your browser at Adobe's Reader support page.

Fig. 7.6 The Help Tool Drop-down Menu

The final option, **Complete Acrobat 7.0 Help**, opens a detailed help system into its own window.

The Edit Toolbar

This toolbar contains buttons that you click to carry out very basic editing functions on comments and text in form fields. The tools on the Advanced Editing toolbar, described later, let you change the actual document text, although in a fairly limited way.

Button   Function

 Spell Check - Check the spelling of any comments or form fields in the current **pdf** document.

 Undo any editing changes you have made. You can **Expand This Button** as shown in Fig. 7.4.

 Redo any editing changes you have made.

 Copy any selected text to the Windows clipboard.

As with the Reader, Acrobat has a couple of toolbar tricks you may find useful:

To select the **Hand** tool temporarily, without deselecting the current tool, hold down the spacebar.

To select the **Zoom In** tool temporarily, press the **Ctrl** key and hold down the **spacebar**.

The Status Bar

The status bar, shown in Fig. 7.7 below, is located at the bottom of the Acrobat window and contains details of a document's status, and buttons to control how a **pdf** file is viewed.

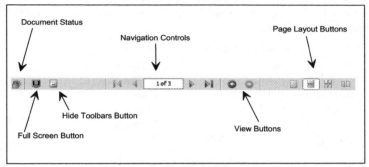

Fig. 7.7 The Adobe Acrobat Status Bar

As all of Acrobat's Status Bar features are the same as those for the Reader, please refer to page 22 onwards for a detailed description of them.

Acrobat Basics

Many of Acrobat's basic features are the same as, or very similar to, those for Adobe Reader. This is not surprising as the Reader is just a 'cut down' version of Acrobat.

So at this stage we suggest you have a look at Chapters 2 and 3 of this book to find out more about the following common features:

8

Using Adobe Acrobat

Setting Preferences

As with Adobe Reader, you can set up Acrobat to work the way you want in the dialogue box, shown in Fig. 8.1 and opened with the **Edit**, **Preferences** menu command, or the **Ctrl+K** shortcut.

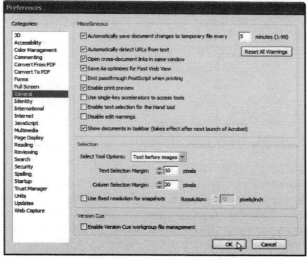

Fig. 8.1 Adobe Acrobat General Preferences

You select the type of preferences from the **Categories** list on the left. As you can see above, 25 categories are available and in our example the General options sheet is open. On each category sheet you select the options you want and when you have finished, click the **OK** button. Clicking **Cancel** will leave the settings unchanged.

Working with pdf Documents

Opening a Document

There are several ways to open and view **pdf** files in Acrobat.

If Acrobat is already open, use the **File**, **Open** menu command, or click the **Open** toolbar button shown here, or use the **Ctrl+O** keyboard shortcut. In the Open dialogue box (Fig. 8.2), select the **pdf** document, or documents, you want to work on, and then click on **Open**.

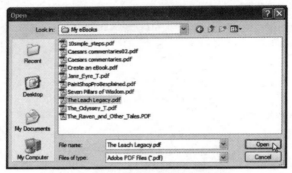

Fig. 8.2 The Open Dialogue Box

If you have used a file very recently you can reopen it from the **File** menu by choosing it from the list at the bottom of the menu. Clicking the **History** option gives you quick access to **pdf** files you have used in the past, as shown in Fig. 8.3 below.

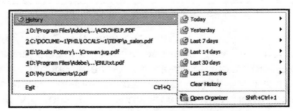

Fig. 8.3 Opening Previous **pdf** Files

As long as Acrobat is set as the default program to open **pdf** files, you can also double-click on a file's icon in a Windows Explorer window to open Acrobat with the file already loaded. If your system opens **pdf** files into another program, such as Adobe Reader, it is very easy to change.

To do this, open a Windows My Computer window and use the **Tools, Folder Options, File Types** command. This will search your system for file associations and after a few moments will open the Folder Options dialogue box shown on the left of Fig. 8.4 below.

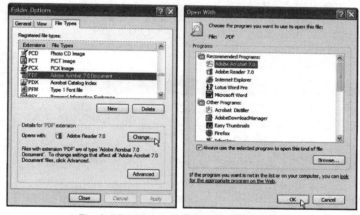

Fig. 8.4 Setting a Windows File Association

Scroll down the list of **Registered file types** and highlight PDF. The panel below will show how your system is set to handle that type of file. In our case, above, **pdf** files were set to open in Adobe Reader. Clicking the **Change** button pointed to above, opens the Open With box, shown on the right of Fig. 8.4. This will list the programs you have installed that can open this type of file. Selecting **Adobe Acrobat** from the list and clicking **OK**, followed by **Close**, will tell Windows to always open a **pdf** file in Adobe Acrobat.

In the future if you want to open a **pdf** file in Reader, just right-click on its icon and select **Open with Adobe Reader 7.0** from the context menu.

When you are 'surfing' on the Internet, you can click a **pdf** link in your web browser. By default, the **pdf** document will open within your web browser. You should then use Acrobat's toolbars to print, search, and work on the document, as the available menu commands will apply to the browser and not to the **pdf** content. If you prefer to have all **pdf**s opening in Acrobat, and not inside your Web browser, have another look at page 38.

Using the Organizer

A new feature to version 7 of Acrobat is the Organizer (sorry about the American spelling). With Organizer, you can see thumbnail images of your **pdf** files to help you quickly find and generally organise them.

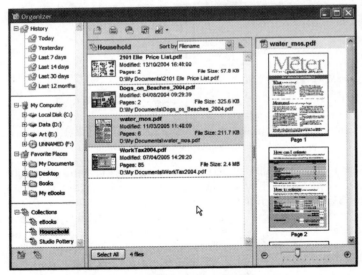

Fig. 8.5 The Organizer Window

 To open the Organizer window click the Organizer button shown here, or use the **File**, **Organizer**, **Open Organizer** menu command.

As shown in Fig. 8.5 on the facing page, there are three panes in the Organizer window. From left to right these are:

Categories pane - This contains four 'categories' to help you locate and organise the **pdf** files on your computer, a network, or even on the Web, (but we haven't tried that)!

*   **History** lists all the **pdf** files that you've opened during a specified period of time.

*   **My Computer** lists the hard drives and folders of your computer for you to locate **pdf** files.

*   **Favorite Places** lists folders, network locations, and Web directories containing **pdf** files. You can add or remove destinations from the Favorite Places list, but you can't edit their names.

*   **Collections** contain **pdf** files that you have associated with each particular collection. A collection folder can point to multiple **pdf** files regardless of where they are located. You can change each collection folder's name and add new ones.

Files pane - This lists the **pdf** files contained in the selected category. In our example, it lists the four files in our Household collection. Each listing in the Files pane displays a thumbnail image of the first page and gives the file's name, its last modification date, the number of pages, the file size and location. You can sort the files using the **Sort by** drop down list. The buttons at the top of the Organizer window let you open a file 🔳, print it 🔳, e-mail it 🔳, combine all selected **pdf** files 🔳, send a selected **pdf** file for review or approval 🔳, or upload it for a browser-based review 🔳.

Pages pane - Displays thumbnails of each page within the **pdf** file selected in the Files pane. The zoom controls at the bottom of the Pages pane let you change the size of the displayed pages. This is fun to play with!

The ability to create collections of similar **pdf** files is the heart of the Organizer. Once done, this makes it very easy to find a file, no matter how complicated your hard disc structure. When first opened, Organizer has three empty collection folders. To rename these, right-click in their name, choose **Rename Collection**, and then type the new name. To delete a collection folder, right-click and choose **Delete Collection**. Don't worry, the files themselves will stay intact! To add a new collection folder, click the **Create a new Collection** button  at the bottom of the pane and type its name.

There are several ways to add a **pdf** file to a collection folder. Perhaps the easiest is to open its folder in the History, My Computer, or Favorite Places category pane, and then drag the **pdf** file from the files pane to the collection folder in the categories pane. You can also drag a **pdf** file straight from a Windows Explorer window to the collection folder in the categories pane.

Another way is to right-click the collection folder name, choose **Add Files** from the context menu, select the **pdf** files to add, and click **Add**.

You can open any **pdf** file from the Organizer window by selecting it in the files pane and clicking the Open button . From Acrobat itself, you can open a **pdf** file from a collection, with the **File**, **Organizer**, **Collections** command, and then choosing the collection name and file name, as shown in Fig. 8.6 below.

Fig. 8.6 Opening a **pdf** Collection File from Acrobat Itself

We find the Organizer a very useful tool for looking after our **pdf** files. If you use it, we are sure you will too. One tip is to minimise the Acrobat window while you are working with the Organizer folders, otherwise the program tends to jump between the two in a very annoying manner.

Document Properties

You can get information about the properties of any **pdf** file such as its title, the fonts it uses, and its security settings. As long as it wasn't originally saved with security settings that prevent changes, you can even change some of a document's properties in Acrobat. To get information about the document currently open in Acrobat, use the **File**, **Document Properties** command, or **Ctrl+D**, to open the dialogue box shown below .

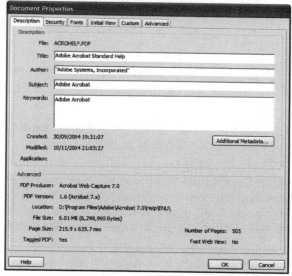

Fig. 8.7 The Document Properties Dialogue Box

This shows the properties of the Acrobat Standard Help file which you should find on your hard disc in the same folder system as the Acrobat program (see **Location** above).

The Description tab, shown open in Fig. 8.7 above, gives basic information about the document, such as its title, author, subject, and keywords. This is known as metadata, and in our example was added by someone at Adobe. If you wanted to, you could change all of these, because as shown in Fig. 8.8 on the next page, no security measures have been placed on the document.

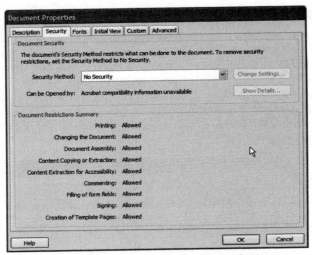

Fig. 8.8 Controlling a Document's Security Settings

The **Help** button on all of these settings sheets gives excellent details of their content, so we will leave it to you to explore them on your own.

The Fonts tab lists the fonts and the font types that were used in the original document (the one the **pdf** was created from). As we shall see later on, it is wise to embed fonts in your documents if they are to be viewed by other people.

In the Initial View tabbed sheet you can control how the document appears when it is opened. We will use these settings after creating an eBook in a later chapter.

Saving pdf Documents

When you create a new **pdf** document, or you modify an existing one in Acrobat, you can save it using the **Save** button, shown here, or the **File**, **Save**, or **File**, **Save As** commands. With the **Save** options, the file is just saved with its current name. With the **Save As** option the dialogue box of Fig. 8.9 is opened and you get more control over the saving operation.

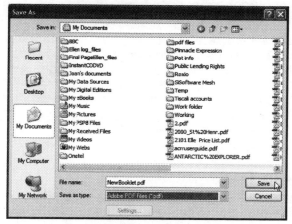

Fig. 8.9 The Save As Dialogue Box

You can use the **Save in** box to select where your document will be saved, and the **File name** box to give your document a name, or change its existing name. To save your document as a **pdf**, you then click the **Save** button.

Converting pdf Documents

If you look closely at the above dialogue box you will see a **Save as type** box and a **Settings** button. These let you convert the open document to one of the different file types shown in Fig. 8.10.

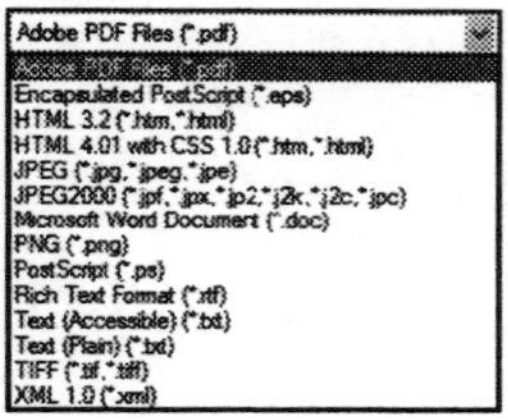

Fig. 8.10 Available Conversion File Types

To convert a file, you click the options button ≋ on the right of the **Save as type** box, choose a file format from the list, and click the **Settings** button to select from the available conversion options. Finally clicking **Save** will convert the **pdf** document and save it in the same folder with the same name but with a new extension, depending on the file type.

Some of the conversion options are out of the scope of this book, so we suggest you look in the Help system under **Converting Adobe PDF documents to other file formats** if you need more details.

If you want to use a **pdf** file in your word processor, you can save it in Microsoft Word Document format (.doc), or in Rich Text Format (.rtf). Be warned though, the new document will not be perfect as coding information is often lost in the conversion. If you convert a **pdf** file to one of the image file formats, (such as .jpg, .png or .tif) each page is saved as a separate image file.

Reducing Document Size

If you want to send a large **pdf** file across the Internet, you can sometimes reduce its file size with the **File**, **Reduce File Size** menu command. Acrobat then resamples the file, recompresses its images, unembeds fonts and sorts out duplicate images and invalid bookmarks. This can reduce the file size considerably, but not unfortunately in all cases.

In this operation you can also reduce a document's file size by limiting the compatibility with earlier versions of Acrobat, as shown in Fig. 8.11 below. To do this though, you must be sure that everyone who will use the file has access to Acrobat 7.0 or Reader 7.0.

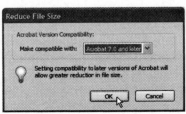

Fig. 8.11 Reducing File Size

Extracting Images

In a similar way, you can also extract all the images from a **pdf** file with the **Advanced**, **Export All Images** menu command. This lets you choose the image type for the saved files as .jpg, .png or .tif, and gives conversion **Settings** as before.

Fig. 8.12 The Export All Images As Dialogue Box

If the file has more than a few images in it, you would be as well opening a new folder for them by clicking the **Create New Folder** button, shown selected in Fig. 8.12 above.

Window Views

Acrobat has more ways for you to view a **pdf** document than the zoom, page rotation and page layout tools, described for Reader at the end of Chapter 2. You can also view different parts of a document at the same time in split or multiple windows

Split Window View

The split window view divides the document pane into either two or four panes with the **Window**, **Split** or **Window**, **Spreadsheet Split** commands.

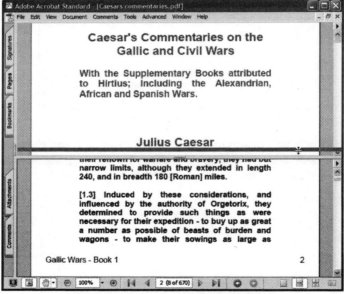

Fig. 8.13 A Document in Window Split View

Split view, shown in Fig. 8.13 above, gives you two independent views of a document. You can scroll, zoom, or turn to a different page in one pane without affecting the other pane at all. You adjust the pane sizes by dragging the divider up or down, as shown above.

The spreadsheet split view splits the Document pane into four panes and can be useful for scrolling through a large spreadsheet or table. In this mode, however, zooming and scrolling affects more than one pane.

With both split views you use the **Window, Remove Split** command to restore the document window to a single pane.

Multiple Windows

Perhaps a better way of working with different parts of a document at the same time is to open multiple windows of it, as shown in Fig. 8.14 below.

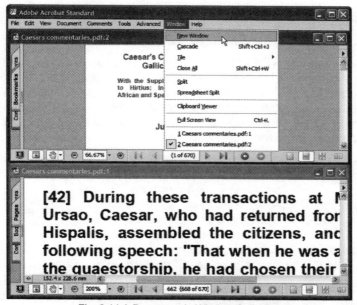

Fig. 8.14 A Document in Window Split View

You can create multiple windows for the same document using the **Window, New Window** command. New windows open at the same page and on top of the original window, but you can then change them how you like. As shown above, Acrobat adds the number suffix 1 to the original file name and increments this suffix for each new window. To close a window, click its close button . The document will stay open as long as at least one window is open.

The **Window** menu, shown open in Fig. 8.14, lets you access open windows and control how they are displayed. In our example, we used the **Window**, **Tile**, **Horizontally** command **(Shift+Ctrl+K)** to have them placed one above the other. To close all open windows for a document, choose **Close All**. You are prompted to save any changes before each window is closed, but Acrobat remains open.

More on Copying Text

As usual with Windows, before you can copy text you must first select it. With Acrobat you use the Select tool, and what you select depends on the page layout that is active. To select text on the current page only, you must set Single Page layout. (See page 24). To select multiple pages of text you use one of the Continuous layouts.

To select text, click the **Select** tool button, click the I pointer at the beginning of the text to be selected, and with the left mouse button depressed, drag to the end of the required text. The selection area turns black while active and the mouse button is depressed. When you release the button the selection colour changes to blue, and the **Copy to Clipboard** icon opens, as in Fig. 8.15. Note the pointers showing the beginning and end of the selection.

Fig. 8.15

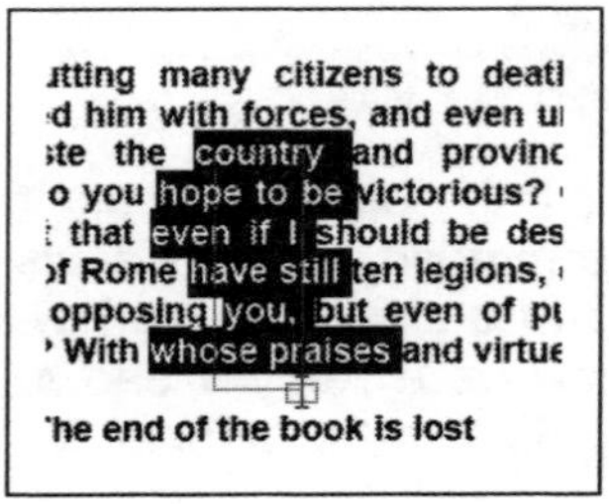

itting many citizens to deati
d him with forces, and even ui
ite the country and provinc
o you hope to be victorious?
t that even if I should be des
of Rome have still ten legions,
opposing you, but even of pi
' With whose praises and virtue

the end of the book is lost

Fig. 8.16 Using the Column-select Pointer

If you move the Select tool pointer around a **pdf** page, you will find it changes shape depending on what it is over. When over text you get the I beam pointer, over an image, it changes to a cross hair -¦- pointer. When over empty space adjacent to text it changes to the Column-select pointer ⌷. As its name suggests, you can use this pointer to select columns, or rectangles, of text as shown in Fig. 8.16, on the previous page. Any words within or intersected by the selection rectangle are selected. You can force this pointer shape anywhere in text by depressing the **Ctrl+Alt** keys.

Double-clicking in a word will select the word. Triple-clicking will select the line of text, and clicking four times will select all the text in a page or the document, depending on the page layout setting (Single Page layout or Continuous layouts respectively). Alternative methods are the **Ctrl+A** keyboard shortcut, or the **Edit**, **Select All** command.

To extend a selection letter by letter, you press **Shift** and an arrow key. To extend a selection word by word, you press **Shift+Ctrl** and the left or right arrow keys. To extend a selection line by line, you press **Shift+Ctrl** and the up or down arrow keys.

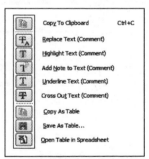

Fig. 8.17 Selection Context Menu

To copy the selected text hold the pointer over the selection until a menu appears, and then choose Copy to Clipboard, which will be the top option. One confusion is that the Copy to Clipboard icon shown in Fig. 8.15 appears when a selection is first made. If you click it then, fine, but it will go as soon as you move the pointer away. The more extended context menu of Fig. 8.17 appears when you next 'hover' the pointer over the selection. Its contents will depend on what is actually selected.

The operations of copying graphics and using the Snapshot tool are the same as described for Reader on pages 57 and 58.

The Clipboard Viewer

As you probably know, when you copy or delete a selection in a Windows application, it is placed on the Windows clipboard. You can then paste it to another location. If you want to see what is actually on the clipboard at any time, you can use the **Windows, Clipboard Viewer** command. In our case this opens the Windows Clipbook Viewer as shown in Fig. 8.18 below

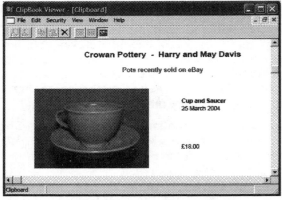

Fig. 8.18 The Windows Clipbook Viewer

This viewer is actually provided with Windows XP and has its own Help system. So having pointed it out, we will leave it to you to explore it further.

The Info Panel

Another Acrobat feature you may find useful is the Info panel, shown in Fig. 8.19 on the facing page. When open, this panel shows the co-ordinates of the mouse pointer within the document pane, with position 0:0 being the top left corner of the current page. The Info panel also shows the width and height of any selection.

You open the Info panel with the **View, Navigation Tabs, Info** command.

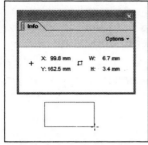

Fig. 8.19 The Info Panel
Shown with a Selection

Here the pointer is at the bottom right of the selection, the X co-ordinate shows this position is 99.8mm from the left edge of the page, the Y shows it is 162.5mm from the top of the page. The selection itself is 6.7mm wide by 3.4mm high.

You can change the units of measurement by clicking the **Options** button. The available units are **Points**, **Inches** and **Millimeters**. Once selected, the Info panel will remain open until you click its close button ▨.

Editing pdf Documents

Acrobat is not designed for creating the content of documents, you do that in other applications like word processors. But you can make minor changes to the text in a **pdf** document using the TouchUp Text tool ▨, which can be found on the Advanced Editing toolbar.

The Advanced Editing Toolbar

This toolbar contains buttons that you can click to change the structure and content of **pdf** documents and text, although sometimes in a fairly limited way.

It is not visible in Acrobat by default, but as we saw on page 103, it can be activated by opening the **View**, **Toolbars** menu, or more easily, by right-clicking in the toolbar area, and ticking the **Advanced Editing** option. Clicking on this list entry will toggle the toolbar on or off.

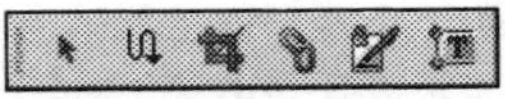

Fig. 8.20 Advanced
Editing Toolbar

Button   Function

Select Object Tool - Used for selecting objects, such as Links, in the current **pdf** document.

Article Tool - Used to create a series of linked rectangles that connect sections of a document and follow the flow of text.

Crop Tool - Used to select the area of a page to keep during a cropping operation, where the page edges are hidden from view. Double-clicking in the selection opens the Crop Pages dialogue box to control the cropping process.

Link Tool - Used to create a Link on a page to somewhere else in the document, to another document, or to a Web site on the Internet.

Digital Signature Field Tool - Used to select the area on a page to place a Digital Signature. A properties box opens for you to complete the operation.

TouchUp Text Tool - Used to edit existing text in the current document, or to add new text.

TouchUp Text Tool

The TouchUp Text tool ▦ can be used to make small changes to the text of a **pdf** document. For large changes you need to use the original application and make a new **pdf** document from it. As well as editing text itself, you can also edit its properties, such as, font type and size, horizontal scale, word and character spacing, character fill and stroke characteristics like colour and line thickness.

To edit text you must have its font installed on your PC. If you don't have the font but it is embedded in the document, you can only change the text properties not the text itself. If the **pdf** file does not allow changes to be made (see Fig. 8.8) the TouchUp Text tool will not be available.

Fig. 8.21 Selecting Text to Edit

You use it by clicking the tool in the text you want to edit. A blue bounding box is placed around the selectable text, as shown in Fig. 8.21.

To add new text, click the I beam pointer where you want it and type the text. In our example, we just typed 'Gaius ' to give Caesar his full name. To edit the text, select it by dragging the pointer over it and type new text to replace the selected text. If you are not happy, just click outside the selection to deselect it and try again.

To edit text attributes, such as font, font size, and letter spacing, first select it, then right-click in the selection, and choose **Properties** from the context menu. This opens the TouchUp Properties dialogue box, shown in Fig. 8.22.

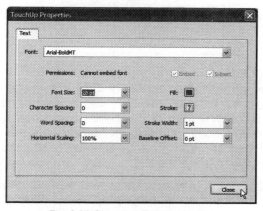

Fig. 8.22 Changing Text Properties

You can change any of the text properties shown above. Clicking the options button ▦ in the **Font** box lets you select any font installed on your system or fully embedded in the document. All the fonts in the file are listed at the top, and those on your computer are listed below. When you have made your changes, click **Close** to implement them.

Adding a Graphic Image

It is very easy to add an image to a **pdf** page once it has been copied to the clipboard. Simply locate the page where you want to place the image, select the **Hand** tool, and use the **Edit**, **Paste** command. This will place the image in the centre of the page. To move it, simply click the image with the pointer and drag it to where you want it, as shown in Fig. 8.23 below.

Fig. 8.23 Relocating a Pasted Image

When you release the mouse button, the image will be moved, but will remain selected, with a square handle at each corner. If you drag one of these corner handles, you can resize the image keeping its aspect ratio, as shown below in Fig. 8.24. With a combination of these actions, you should be able to place the image just where you want it.

If you double-click the new image you will find that Acrobat considers it to be a document 'stamp', part of the document

review process. We do not cover that in this book, but it is still a useful way to place an image on a page!

Fig. 8.24 Resizing an Image

Manipulating Document Pages

The rest of this chapter is devoted to techniques you may need when dealing with large **pdf** documents, such as reports, books or eBooks.

Cropping Pages

There may be times when the size of the pages that make up a document are not consistent, or the software that was used to create the **pdf** could not generate custom page sizes, only A4. In these cases you need to crop the pages to the correct size. In our example below, the latter is the case and the actual page size is shown by crop marks, added by the word processor during the printing process. When the **pdf** is sent to the book printers this is no problem, but if we want to create an eBook we have to crop the pages.

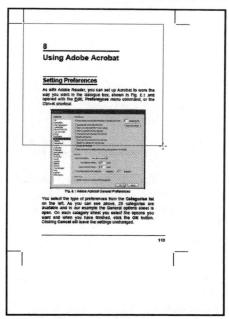

Fig. 8.25 Using the Crop Selection Tool

With cropping, information is not discarded from a **pdf** file, but just hidden from view. You can access it later if you want.

Before cropping, click the Single Page layout button 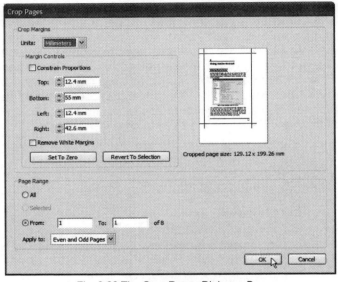 on the status bar. Then we prefer to use the Crop tool 🎨 on the Advanced Editing Toolbar to select the area of page that we want to display, as shown in Fig. 8.25 on the previous page. Double-clicking in the selection, opens the Crop Pages dialogue box shown below.

Fig. 8.26 The Crop Pages Dialogue Box

If necessary, you can adjust the **Top**, **Bottom**, **Left**, and **Right** margins by entering values or clicking the increment arrows ▓. The **Constrain Proportions** option adjusts all the margins at the same time. The **Page Range** options let you crop any pages you want in the document at the same time.

When you are happy with your choices click the **OK** button to carry out the crop. At any time in the future you can reverse the cropping operation, by opening the Crop Pages dialogue box again and clicking the **Set to Zero** button.

Page Numbers

In Acrobat and Reader, page numbers are shown on the status bar below the document in the Document pane and under each thumbnail image in the Pages pane. By default these numbers are shown in logical order, 1, 2, 3.... But with large documents you often have different sections that you want to number separately, like in Fig. 8.27 below.

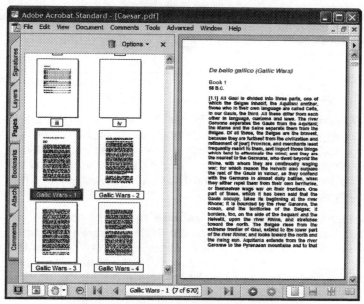

Fig. 8.27 An eBook with Acrobat Page Numbers Set

Here we have numbered the eBook's introductory pages with a 'i, ii, iii...' number sequence (after leaving the two cover pages unnumbered). The book's first main section has the text preface 'Gallic Wars - ' placed in front of the section page number, which was set to start at 1.

This may look complicated, but is very easy to do. Once you have decided on your sections, highlight all the pages of a section in the Pages pane, and at the top of the pane, click the **Options** button. This opens the menu shown in Fig. 8.28 on the next page.

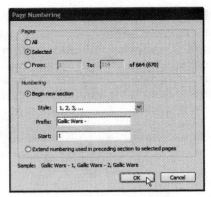

Fig. 8.28 The Page Pane
Options Menu

Fig. 8.29 The Page Numbering
Dialogue Box

Choosing **Number Pages** in the Options menu (pointed to above) opens the Page Numbering dialogue box shown in Fig. 8.29. The **Selected** option will already be active as long as you selected the pages in the Pages pane. If not, you will have to do it manually in the **From** and **To** boxes, which is much more fiddly!

Leave the **Begin new section** option selected in the **Numbering** section and open the **Style** pull-down list, shown in Fig. 8.30, to choose a page numbering style. Our example

Fig. 8.30
Numbering
Styles

in Fig. 8.29 shows the entries made to create the page numbers shown in Fig. 8.27. This figure also shows that the new page numbers display on the status bar below the document and under each thumbnail image in the Pages pane, but not on the document itself. To do that, they need to be set in a Footer, as described next.

It is usually preferable to remove page numbers from your source material before converting it to **pdf**. The Acrobat page numbering is then easier to do and there will not be any conflicting numbers.

Headers and Footers

Now we can assign page numbers to our documents, we need to know about headers and footers before we can put printable numbers on the document pages. In Acrobat you can add precise headers and footers to the pages, as we show below in the same eBook as before.

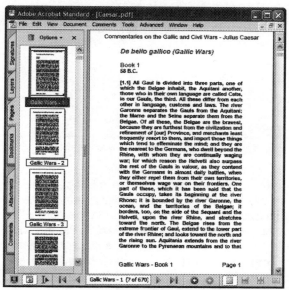

Fig. 8.31 An eBook with a Header and Footers

In this example we have added a header to the top of each page, and two footers to the bottom. The one on the right just holds the page number, as we shall see.

If you are going to add headers or footers to a **pdf**, make sure they don't clash with ones that were added to the source document. In fact it is probably better to remove them from the source document before the **pdf** is created in the first place.

To add headers or footers use the **Document, Add Headers & Footers** command to open the Add Headers & Footers dialogue box shown in Fig. 8.32 on the next page.

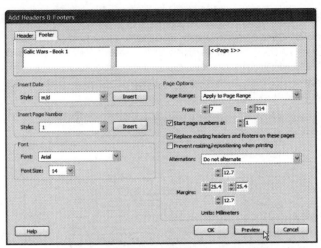

Fig. 8.32 Adding Footers to a Document Section

At the top of the dialogue box are three header boxes and three footer boxes, each on its own tabbed sheet. Anything placed in the left boxes will be left justified on the page, in the middle boxes will be centred, and in the right will be right justified. Above, we just typed our text in the left footer box, clicked in the right box and chose a page numbering style from the **Style** pull-down list for **Insert Page Number**.

Next, we clicked the Header tab and typed our text into the centre box. The **Font** and **Font Size** options apply to all headers and footers you place in a session. At any time you can click the **Preview** button to see what your pages will look like. Clicking on **OK** will apply the headers and footers to the pages specified in the **Page Range** section.

To modify headers or footers use the **Document**, **Add Headers & Footers** command again and make your changes. Make sure the **Replace existing headers and footers on these pages** option is checked. If you want to delete a header or footer, just delete the text in its text box and click **OK** to close the dialogue box. The header or footer will disappear.

9

About eBooks

What are eBooks?

eBooks are electronic books designed to be read on a computer screen or some other hand-held device. There are several eBook formats in use, **pdf** being one of the main ones. EBooks in **pdf** maintain the feel of traditional book pages, making reading and browsing quite intuitive. Page numbers and tables of contents can be preserved, providing a familiar reading experience.

Electronic publishing is still in its infancy as, let's face it, many people are not too happy with computers, let alone abandoning books for them! We think eBooks are here to stay, not as a replacement (yet) for paper books but as a complement to the printed word.

Advantages of eBooks

eBooks take up no physical space apart from that on your hard-drive. You can store your own personal library on your PC, Laptop or hand-held device.

They can be almost instantly transmitted over the Internet, with minimal replication and distribution costs. You can download eBooks in minutes and read them immediately, so there is no waiting for shipment and in most cases, they are cheaper than their paper counterparts. Some can even be free.

The ability to quickly and comprehensively search eBooks for specific text is another advantage. Using a paper book's index now seems very primitive compared with your computer scanning through a **pdf** eBook for particular words or concepts. Also, the ability to follow links through an eBook, like you do on a Web site, adds to the reading experience. In an eBook, clicking directly on a page can let you look up the meanings of words, or explore cross-references in the same book, other books on your computer, or even on the Internet. You can also activate multimedia content such as sound, video, and animation.

The downside to all this is that eBooks you buy usually have security settings which prevent or limit printing and copying, and often stop you using the book on more than one device.

Digital Editions

Adobe in their wisdom now call eBooks 'Digital Editions'. Until recently they operated a Media Store where you could buy **pdf** eBooks, but according to their Web site, "we closed it due to the success of online retailers in the current market, there no longer being a need for Adobe to support a separate **pdf** store". We prefer the name eBook so will carry on using it!

Where to Get eBooks

Most eBooks available from commercial Web sites are the same as the ones you find in traditional book shops, such as novels, biographies, business books, etc. If you do an Internet search for 'eBook' you will uncover hundreds of places that sell them. The main ones for **pdf** format are:

www.amazon.co.uk
www.ebooks.com
ebooks.whsmith.co.uk
ebooks.efollett.com
www.fictionwise.com
www.powells.com/ebookstore/ebooks.html

eBooks, though, can include printed information of all kinds, such as newspapers and periodicals, reference works, technical manuals, journals, business documents, and rare or out-of-print books that have been scanned in **pdf** format.

A good place to start is Project Gutenberg which with over 15,000 probably has the largest single collection of free eBooks anywhere. Michael Hart, its founder, 'invented' eBooks in 1971. The project use hundreds of volunteers to produce their books, most of which are older literary works from the public domain in the United States. They can all be freely downloaded, and redistributed for non-commercial use from their Web site:

www.gutenberg.org

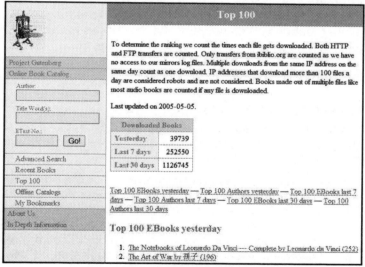

Fig. 9.1 Project Gutenberg's Top 100 Page

This is a very comprehensive and easy to use site. Their eBooks are available for download in **pdf** format and as **.txt** files. Some of the example eBooks we have used in earlier chapters were created from downloaded text files. We enjoy making our own eBooks, and most of the rest of this book is devoted to just that.

Reading eBooks

To read **pdf** eBooks, all you need is a copy of Adobe Reader on your PC. If necessary, we suggest you go back to Chapters 2 to 5 to find out more about this excellent software. It enables you to read top quality eBooks as well as other **pdf** files, and displays them with the same pictures, graphics, and fonts you would get in your printed books.

With Reader, eBooks published in **pdf** can be instantly searched, electronically annotated with a variety of mark-up tools, and scaled to fit the viewing area of your reading device.

The automatic scrolling feature, activated with the **View**, **Automatically Scroll** menu command or **Shift+Ctrl+H**, makes it easier to scan through eBooks (see page 80). Another feature you may find useful for eBooks is the **View**, **Read Out Loud** command, described on page 68.

Activating Adobe Reader

In order to read digitally protected **pdf**s (like the Adobe eBooks found at commercial sites), you may need to activate your copy of Adobe Reader.

'E-Z Activation' will automatically take place the first time you download and attempt to open a digitally protected **pdf**. Once E-Z Activation is complete, your browser will display the Adobe DRM Activator screen, and hopefully tell you that activation was successful. You will be prompted to complete a process called Named Activation. If you intend to use Adobe eBooks on multiple machines, you should follow the steps to do this.

If you don't, you can complete Named Activation at any time from the Adobe Reader menu bar, by selecting **File**, **Digital Editions**, **Authorize Devices**. Your browser will open the Adobe DRM Activator Site Web site for you to activate your copy of Adobe Reader. Good luck.

Using Adobe Reader

Once you have started the eBook process with Adobe Reader you will find a new button on the Tasks toolbar, as shown here.

This is the **Read a Digital Edition** button. Clicking it opens the drop-down menu shown in Fig. 9.2. The **How To...** Option should not be necessary now, and the **Adobe Digital Media Store** is no longer open. **Authorize Devices** is

Fig. 9.2 Digital Edition Menu

another way of starting the software activation procedure, described on the previous page. The most useful option on this menu is **My Digital Editions**, which opens the window shown in Fig. 9.3 below.

Fig. 9.3 The My Digital Editions Window

My Digital Editions

This is the bookshelf, which shows the contents of your eLibrary as a series of thumbnails ▦ (or as a list of book titles with author and other information ▤). When you select a thumbnail, the eBook title, author, number of pages, publisher and ISBN number, appears at the bottom of the window, as shown above. You can also open the bookshelf with the **File**, **Digital Editions**, **My Digital Editions** command and close it by clicking the **Close** button.

When you download a **pdf** eBook the file is usually placed in either the 'My eBooks' folder or 'My Digital Editions' folder, which can be found in the My Documents folder. The book details may also be placed in My Digital Editions. If not, you can use the **Add File** button [Add File] to select any eBooks from your hard discs that you want included.

To open an eBook for reading, select its thumbnail and click the [Read] button, or just double-click the thumbnail. You can also open an eBook straight from Reader with the **File**, **Open** command, or straight from its Windows folder by double-clicking its icon or name. With the latter method Reader (or Acrobat, depending on your setup) is opened with the eBook active.

Safeguarding your eBooks

It is good practice to create backup copies of your downloaded eBooks (and other **pdf** files) in case you delete them by mistake, your hard disc crashes, or even worse you lose your hardware. You can back up any of the files you have stored in the My Digital Editions bookshelf by clicking the Backup button [Backup], and choosing what to backup from the menu that opens. You can even save any comments and markups that you have made in your eBooks. You would normally choose to backup your eBooks to a CD drive. To restore an eBook in the future, put the CD in its drive, click the **Backup** button, select **Restore**, find the folder that contains the file you want to restore, and click **OK**.

You can also save a copy of an individual eBook with the **Save A Copy** button [Save a Copy].

To remove an eBook from the My Digital Editions bookshelf, right-click its thumbnail, and select **Remove** from the context menu that opens. This doesn't delete the eBook from your system it just removes it from the bookshelf.

Planning an eBook

In the next chapter we cover several techniques for creating eBooks using Adobe Acrobat. Before we get to that, we will cover some basic guidelines to ensure the eBooks you create 'from scratch' are both easy to read and foolproof.

A Page Template

The standard page size for most people's printed pages is A4, or maybe the American 'Letter' size which is a little bit smaller. For eBooks this is not ideal, as you cannot view a whole page on screen and still read the text comfortably. If you create an eBook from a word processed document, you should create a special page template in your word processor. Adobe recommend the following:

Page Size - For most eBooks a page size of 6 inch by 9 inch is ideal. Pages of this size can be comfortably displayed on a variety of devices and can be easily printed.

Page Margins - Margins help readers follow the text and rest their eyes when needed. To make dense pages more inviting, you should set ample margins that reduce the amount of text and images cramped on each page. We use 1 inch margins all around the page, but you may prefer 1.5 inch left and right margins. Make sure you use the same margins throughout the eBook, or the text will appear to jump from left to right as you scan through the book in Reader.

Text - You should choose fonts that look good on screen and are easy to read. Fonts with delicate serifs may look good on paper but can lose their definition on screen, which makes them difficult to read. For maximum readability at 100% magnification in Reader, for body text we use the Arial font at a size of 12 points and a leading of 2 points.

Colour - This does not cost any extra in an eBook, so you should consider using colour images and adding colour to headings and captions.

Some Basic Rules

If your eBooks are to be published, or even used by other people, you should make sure they will display correctly on other computers and devices.

If at all possible, create the eBook **pdf** file on the same computer as the original document was created. This will ensure that the fonts needed to create, view, and print the **pdf** file will be available.

Always Embed Fonts - This will ensure that the **pdf** file always has the information necessary to faithfully re-create the characters used in your **pdf** file. If a font is not embedded and is not available on the computer reading the eBook, another font will be substituted. The results then may be very different from what you planned! To do this you need to customise your Adobe PDF Settings (page 84), which is covered in the next chapter.

Check the Results - You should check how your eBook displays on a computer other than the one used to create it with the local fonts turned off. In Acrobat, use the **Advanced**, **Use Local Fonts** command. When Use Local Fonts is not selected it does not have a check mark by it and Acrobat displays the **pdf** file using substitute fonts for all fonts that are not embedded. If you have a font problem it should soon come to light. The text in your **pdf** file will not display correctly, or appear as bullets. In this case the fonts will not have been properly embedded.

It's also a good idea to check the readability of your text under a variety of conditions, including both CRT and LCD displays.

10

Making eBooks

There are several techniques for getting data, or information, into **pdf** format to form the content of an eBook, or a large **pdf** document. Apart from the first ones discussed below, many of the rest depend on you having Adobe Acrobat.

Using a Word Processor

The main technique, which we have touched on several times so far, is to create and format the text and graphic content in a word processor, or desk top publishing package. Microsoft Word would probably be the most common application here, although we also use Lotus WordPro.

The actual eBook content we can't help you with! Maybe it's the novel you have always wanted to see in print, maybe a text book, maybe a book like ours. If you want to try, but are not feeling too original, why not visit Project Gutenberg (see page 141) and find an out of copyright book you would like to read and play with. Follow their instructions and download it as a text file. Once it is on your computer you can, within reason, do what you want with it. But first make sure you read the header which contains their conditions of use.

In your word processor, create your eBook template with the features described on page 145. How you do this depends on the word processor you are using, so we can't really help here either. If necessary, you could look at the book list on page ii, we may have covered this elsewhere, maybe *Microsoft Office 2003 explained* or an earlier version might help.

Starting with a new blank document using your eBook template and the correct page size, either type in your text, open a text file, or copy and paste it from another source.

Removing Paragraph Marks

You should very rapidly then be able to reformat the text into the styles you want for your eBook. If you have imported a text file, you may have the problem of a paragraph mark at the end of each line of text. This will make reformatting the text impossible, but is easy to solve.

Using the **Find and Replace** function of your word processor, replace double paragraph marks with something that is not in the text, we use '***'. Then replace single paragraph marks with a 'space' character. Finally replace '***' with double paragraph marks. Most of your text should now be OK; you may have to do a little bit of manual editing to tidy it up. If anything goes wrong, don't forget you can use the **Undo** feature to cancel out a document change.

Using Headers and Footers

Once you have your book properly formatted and looking how you want it to, you must decide whether to add page numbers and headers or footers in your word processor, or later in Acrobat when your document is converted to **pdf** (see Chapter 8). Of course, if you don't have Acrobat and are using a substitute program to create your **pdf**, you will have to do everything in your word processor.

Converting to pdf

In Chapter 6 we looked at a range of ways to convert a word processed file to a **pdf**. Which method you use now will depend on which software you decide on. Make sure you use the best conversion settings for screen and Internet use.

Adobe pdf Settings

If you are using Acrobat to make your conversion to **pdf**, you should make a custom settings for eBooks for Acrobat Distiller to use. In fact the **Smallest File Size** default settings are almost ideal, so we recommend a small change to this.

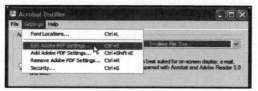

Fig. 10.1 Editing PDF Settings in Distiller

Open Distiller, as described on page 84, select **Smallest File Size** in the **Default Settings** box, and then choose **Settings**, **Edit Adobe PDF Settings** from the Distiller menu, as shown in Fig. 10.1 above. This opens the Adobe PDF Settings dialogue box shown in Fig. 10.2.

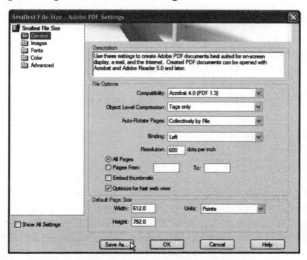

Fig. 10.2 Editing General Settings in Distiller

We suggest you make your eBook compatible with Acrobat 4.0 or later, so that users with older versions of Reader will be able to access it, but some colour features will not be lost.

To do this, select Acrobat 4.0 from the **Compatibility** drop-down list, as we have done in Fig. 10.2. At this stage, this is probably the only change you need to make to the settings. Click the **Save As** button and save the new settings sheet as **eBook**. The file suffix **.joboptions** will be added by Acrobat.

Now, whenever you are about to convert a word processed file to **pdf,** make sure you select the new eBooks settings in the Default Settings box of whatever Acrobat tool you use. One thing to remember is that Distiller uses the settings that were active the last time it was used, so you must check this if you make different types of **pdf** documents.

If in the future you find you need to change any of the other settings, maybe to reduce file size at the expense of image quality, just experiment with different settings, until you get the result you want.

The Conversion

How you actually convert the file to **pdf** will depend on what program you are using. We discussed this in some depth in Chapter 6 so, if necessary, please go back and have another look.

Using a Scanner

It is quite easy with Acrobat to make an electronic copy of pages, or even whole books. Many libraries let you access **pdf** versions of their books, especially valuable antique books. For most of us, that is the only way we will ever get access to them. Please bear in mind that most books are copyrighted and making electronic copies is usually frowned upon! So be warned.

There are two main ways of creating eBooks with a scanner. One is to scan each page as a graphic image, and the other is to scan straight into Acrobat.

Scanning Page Images

We find this method preferable if the pages contain high quality graphics mixed with text, especially if we want to maintain or even edit the quality of pages. It involves scanning each page wanted in the **pdf** at a resolution of 300 dpi (dots per inch). With lower resolutions, Acrobat may have trouble recognising the text at a later stage. This operation is shown for one of our scanners in Fig. 10.3 below.

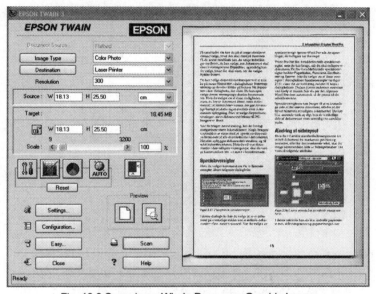

Fig. 10.3 Scanning a Whole Page as a Graphic Image

Your scanner software may well be different, but this shows the main settings used. Each page is saved as a graphic image. We usually carry out the scanning from Paint Shop Pro which lets us edit the scanned images and we then save them as **.png** images. The editing can remove marks or discolouration from the pages and let you accurately control the page size. If you need more information here, we suggest you try our book *Paint Shop Pro 8 explained*, also published by Babani (publishing).

Combining the Pages

When you have finished scanning all the pages, and hopefully saved them in their own folder, you need to combine them all into one **pdf** file. This you do in Acrobat, with the **File**, **Create PDF**, **From Multiple Files** command, or by selecting **Multiple Files** from the Create PDF tool menu, shown earlier in Fig. 6.10. This opens the Create PDF from Multiple Documents dialogue box shown below.

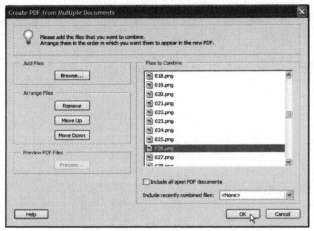

Fig. 10.4 Selecting Files to Combine into a **pdf** File

Here we clicked the **Browse** button and selected the files for each page of the eBook from the Open dialogue box.

Files are converted and joined in the order shown in the above list, so it is important to make sure they are in the correct order. You can drag files within the list, or move a file up or down the list, by selecting it and clicking the **Move Up** or **Move Down** buttons. The **Remove** button does just that to a selected file. When the list is how you want it, click **OK** and Acrobat converts and consolidates the files into one Adobe **pdf** file, as shown here in Fig. 10.5.

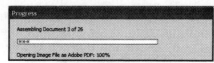

Fig. 10.5 Assembling a Document

When the conversion is complete, the consolidated **pdf** file opens in Acrobat, and you are very forcefully prompted to save the file as Binder1.pdf. You can obviously change this name to something more meaningful if you prefer.

You now have a **pdf** file made up of all your scanned pages, hopefully in the correct order. The only problem is that you will also have a very big file, so this method is not really suitable for creating eBooks to publish over the Internet. However, for your own use from a hard disc, or from a CD or DVD, file size is not a problem.

Recognising Text

Now for the clever bit. The reason the file is so large is because we scanned at a resolution of 300dpi. For use on a computer screen, a resolution of 75dpi would have been adequate, and would have produced a much smaller file size. BUT we want to be able to recognise the text in the eBook using OCR software (Optical Character Recognition) built into Acrobat, and this only works well with higher resolution scans. OCR software enables you to search and copy, and in some cases, correct the text in a scanned **pdf** file.

To convert your scanned pages to searchable text, open the file in Acrobat, and use the **Document** , **Recognize Text Using OCR**, **Start** menu command. This opens the dialogue box shown in Fig. 10.6 in which you specify the pages to be converted. If the **Settings** are different from those shown here, click the **Edit** button and change them. The **PDF Output Style: Searchable Image (Exact)** option, shown here, keeps a bitmap image of the eBook

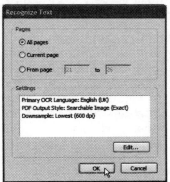

Fig. 10.6 Recognising Text

pages in the foreground with the converted text on an invisible layer beneath. The other settings here, you can explore yourself in the Help system. Click **OK** to start the OCR scan. If the file has a lot of pages, now is a good time to make a cup of coffee, or put a bet on a horse.

All being well, in a few minutes (or hours depending on your PC and the number of pages involved) the scan will finish and control will be returned to you. Your pages will look very much the same, except for the odd one being straightened out, but your text will now be selectable and searchable. Don't forget to save the file again, or you may have to repeat the whole performance! For details on searching **pdf** files see page 44.

This technique can make a very useful research tool out of these publications you are always having to refer to, as it is very quick, easy and powerful to use Acrobat or Reader searches. But, once again, watch your copyrights.

Scanning from Acrobat

Another method of creating a **pdf** file from paper copy is to let Acrobat control the actual scanning process. This method is much quicker than the previous, but you don't get the option to edit the pages. Acrobat does try very hard to give you good scan results though.

In Acrobat, choose **File**, **Create PDF**, **From Scanner**, or select **From Scanner** from the Create PDF tool menu, shown earlier in Fig. 6.10. This opens the Create PDF from

Scanner box shown here in Fig. 10.7. Select your **Scanner** and whether to **Scan** Both Sides or Front Sides.

Fig. 10.7 Scanner Settings

If you are going to scan a range of pages from a book, use the Front Sides setting. If no **pdf** document is open in Acrobat, the **Destination** menu is unavailable, as in our example (Fig. 10.7). If you have a **pdf** open you can choose to create a new document or to append your scans to the already open document.

Fig. 10.8 Changing Text Settings

Make sure that **Recognize Text Using OCR** is selected so that Acrobat recognises each page of text as it is converted to **pdf**. The **Settings** button opens the dialogue box shown here in Fig. 10.8.

You should probably change **Primary OCR Language** to English (UK) and specify options. **PDF Output Style** has two options, either Searchable Image or Formatted Text & Graphics. Searchable Image, as in our last section, produces a bitmap image of the pages with the scanned and recognised text on an invisible layer below, the text being selectable and readable. The Formatted Text & Graphics option rebuilds the scanned page using recognised text, fonts, pictures, and other graphic elements. You can correct this if text recognition is incorrect. Downsample Images decreases the number of pixels in scanned images.

The **Image Settings** button on the Create PDF from Scanner dialogue box (Fig. 10.7) lets you set compression and filtering options to optimise the scan results. We will leave it to you to play with these settings. Clicking the **Scan** button passes control to your scanner software, as long as the scanner is switched on, of course.

For OCR to work properly we recommend scanning at a resolution of 300dpi. With lower resolutions, Acrobat has more trouble recognising the text. The settings for one of our scanners is shown on the next page in Fig. 10.9. Your scanner software will almost certainly be different, so don't expect to see the same scanner window as ours.

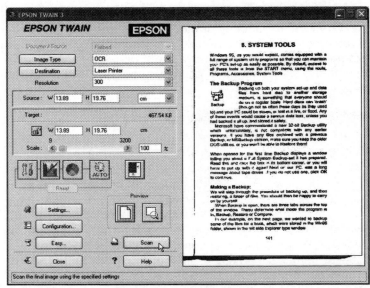

Fig. 10.9 Scanner Control Settings

In our case, we select the scanner settings and the area of the page to scan and click the **Scan** button, but your scan actions may not be the same. Acrobat then takes over again and imports the scan data, converts it to **pdf**, and OCR recognises the text on the page. When it is ready you will be asked for instructions in a message box similar to that in Fig. 10.10. Click **Next** to carry on scanning, or if you have finished click the **Done** button.

Fig. 10.10
Instruction Box

As described, this method may sound a little tedious, but Adobe have in Version 7.0 of Acrobat, produced a very easy way to scan long documents into the **pdf** format. This method is especially useful for archiving paper documents, and must be classed as a move towards the fictional 'paper-less office'.

Now you have your eBook written and compiled in **pdf** format it is time to fine tune its display and presentation.

Working with pdf Pages

Fig. 10.11 Pages Options Menu

In Acrobat, as with Reader, Page thumbnails provide miniature previews of document pages. You can use them to change the display in the document pane and to go to other pages in the document. When the Pages tab is open you jump to another page by clicking the page's thumbnail. But with Acrobat, the **Options** drop-down menu at the top of the Pages tab has far more power, as shown in Fig. 10.11.

As with Reader, it allows you to reduce and enlarge the size of the page thumbnails in the pane, but it also has a range of commands that let you manipulate the actual pages in a **pdf** document. Many of these options can also be found in Acrobat's **Document** menu.

Inserting Pages

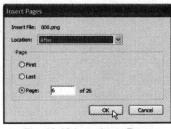

Fig. 10.12 Inserting a Page

To insert pages anywhere in your document, select the thumbnail of the page before the insertion point, click the **Options** button and choose **Insert Pages**. Select the page, or pages, you want to insert in the box that opens. You may need to change the **Files of type** setting in order to find them. Clicking the **Select** button opens the Insert Pages dialogue box shown here in Fig. 10.12.

In this box you control whether the insertion is placed Before, or After, the **First** or **Last** page, or a particular **Page**. As usual, click on **OK** to carry out the operation. If you select file types other than **pdf**, Acrobat converts the pages to **pdf** before inserting them.

Extracting Pages

Fig. 10.13 Extracting a Page

To extract pages from your document, select the page thumbnails to extract, click the **Options** button and choose **Extract Pages**. This opens the box shown in Fig. 10.13.

To remove the pages from the document, just select **Delete Pages After Extracting** and click **OK**. To save the pages as a new file but leave the original pages in place, just select **Extract Pages As Separate Files** and click **OK**. To remove the selected pages and save them as a new file select both options and click **OK**.

Replacing Pages

You can replace one or more pages of your document with pages from another **pdf** document. To do this, open both documents with their Pages tabs showing and have them displayed on your screen at the same time. Select the page thumbnails you want to use as replacement pages, or drag a rectangle around them, and then drag the selection onto the Pages tab of your target document. Position the ‎ pointer directly over the page number box of the first page thumbnail you want to replace, as shown in Fig. 10.14, and release the mouse button.

The pages you selected in the first document will replace the highlighted pages in the second document, starting at the page number you select. Needless to say, you need to take care with this operation!

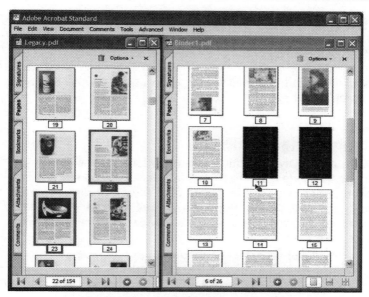

Fig. 10.14 Replacing Pages in a Document

In our example above, we have selected pages 22 and 23 of the left hand document, and are using them to replace pages 11 and 12 of the document on the right.

Deleting Pages

To delete pages, simply select their thumbnails and press the **Delete** key on the keyboard. You can also choose **Delete Pages** from the Options menu, which opens the

Fig. 10.15 Deleting a Page

Delete Pages dialogue box shown here in Fig. 10.15. You can also click the 🗑 **Trash can** button at the top of the pane to delete selected thumbnails. The choice is yours. Be careful though, because you can't undo a **Delete** command, but they all give you a fail-safe warning message, and you have to click **OK** before the operation is carried out.

Navigation Controls

One of the advantages of eBooks is the ease with which you can navigate through them, mainly by clicking bookmarks and links. But this facility has to be added by the author, it doesn't just happen.

Embedding Thumbnails

One easy way of getting around a large file is by clicking page thumbnails in the Pages tab pane we spent some time with in the last section. If you click the **Options** button and choose **Embed All Page Thumbnails**, (see Fig. 10.11), Acrobat will embed a thumbnail preview for each page in the file, as shown below.

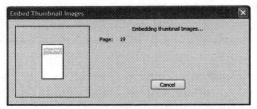

Fig. 10.16 Embedding Thumbnails into a **pdf** File

Embedding thumbnails increases the file size and the images produced are of fairly poor quality, so you are probably better off not doing this with your eBook. In fact, Acrobat and Reader 5.0, and later versions, generate thumbnails automatically whenever you click the Pages tab, so they would only be of real use for older versions.

Adding Bookmarks

Bookmarks are another matter altogether. They are used to jump to a destination within the current **pdf** document, to another document, or to a Web page. Bookmarks can also be set to perform actions. At a minimum, you should prepare a table of contents at the beginning of your eBook, or long

pdf document. Each entry in this table should be used as a bookmark, so that when it is clicked, the page concerned is opened in the document pane. For some eBooks you may also consider treating the index entries in the same way. To do this you need to use links, discussed in the next section.

If you generated a table of contents in your word processor when you prepared the source document, then you may be lucky. When Acrobat creates a **pdf** document, bookmarks are generated automatically from the table of contents entries of documents created by many programs. If not, you will have to do it manually, as we show below.

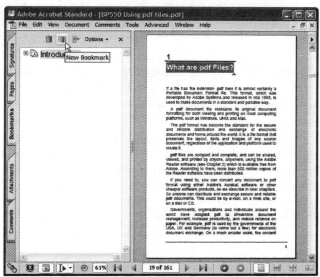

Fig. 10.17 Adding a New Bookmark

In Fig. 10.17 we have the Bookmarks tab open and have already placed one bookmark. The destination page for the next bookmark is open and we have set the document view we want.

To set the next bookmark, make sure the Select tool 📳 is active and drag it to select the bookmark text. In our case the chapter title, which becomes the label of the new bookmark. In the Bookmarks tab, click the bookmark under which you want to place the new bookmark, and finally click the **New Bookmark** button pointed to in Fig. 10.17. If necessary, edit the name of the new bookmark, as we show in Fig. 10.18, and press the **Enter** key.

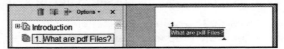

Fig. 10.18 Editing the New Bookmark

Leave the new bookmark selected and locate the next destination in the document pane. Highlight its text and repeat the above procedure. This will produce a new bookmark below the first, as in Fig. 10.19 (a) below.

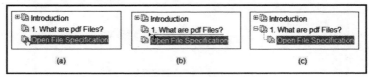

Fig. 10.19 Nesting a Bookmark

In our example the new bookmark needs to be a sub-category of the one above it. To nest a bookmark into another bookmark group, select it and drag its icon directly under the parent bookmark, as shown in (b) above. The dotted line icon shows the position. Release the mouse button and the bookmark will be nested, as in (c) above.

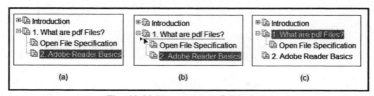

Fig. 10.20 Un-nesting a Bookmark

Fig. 10.20 above, shows the operation of moving a bookmark up one level in the nesting hierarchy. You click the bookmark (a), and drag the ▶ pointer so that the dotted line is under the whole of the correct bookmark in the above list (b). Releasing the mouse button un-nests the bookmark, (c).

When we started, it took us a few goes to get this right, so be prepared for some trial and error here.

To expand a bookmark, and show its nestlings, you click the plus sign ⊞ next to it. To collapse it again, click the minus sign ⊟. To delete a bookmark, select it and choose **Delete**

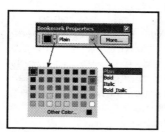

Fig. 10.21 Properties Bar

Bookmark(s) from the Options menu, or click the **Delete Selected Bookmarks** button ▦ , on the tab at the top of the pane.

You can choose a colour and style for the text of a selected bookmark from the Properties toolbar shown in Fig. 10.21. This is opened with the **View**, **Toolbars**, **Properties Bar** menu command, or the **Ctrl+E** keyboard shortcut. Once you have set the appearance of one bookmark, you can use the same settings for others by right-clicking the bookmark and choosing the **Use Current Appearance As New Default** option from the context menu.

The **More** button on the Bookmark Properties toolbar (Fig. 10.21) opens the Bookmark Properties dialogue box shown in Fig. 10.22 with the Actions tab active. You can also

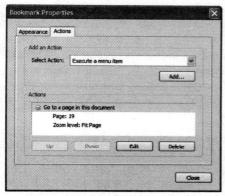

Fig. 10.22 Bookmark Properties

right-click a bookmark, and choose **Properties** to open this box, or use the **Ctrl+I** keyboard shortcut. In the Actions tab section of this dialogue box, you can choose an action from the **Select Action** drop-down menu, shown in Fig. 10.23 on the next page, and click **Add**.

Fig. 10.23 Actions Menu

The selected action will then be carried out when the bookmark is clicked. As shown here, the list of possible actions is quite extensive.

When you first open the Bookmark tab of your new eBook, you may find a range of bookmarks has already been placed by Acrobat when the **pdf** was created. If so, you may only have to edit the text on these bookmarks, or change their destinations. To edit a bookmark's destination, first select the bookmark and in Acrobat's document pane, move to the new destination location. If necessary, reset the view magnification, click the **Options** button and choose **Set Bookmark Destination**.

With a little bit of experimenting, you should now be able to work your way through your eBook, putting bookmarks wherever necessary. If you get stuck, there is always the Help system. Look in the 'Using Bookmarks' section.

Adding Links

Clicking a link in a **pdf** document is like clicking a link on a Web page. Links can take you to another location in the current document, to other documents, or even to Web sites on the Internet. There are several places you should seriously consider putting links in your eBooks. If your source document contained an index and contents page(s), they will be in your **pdf** document but, as they are, will not be very much help to your readers. But, if you link all of their entries to the relevant page of the book, that will be a different matter altogether.

To do this, you should first open Acrobat's Advanced Editing toolbar (see page 129) by right-clicking in the toolbar area, and ticking the **Advanced Editing** option. Select the Link tool ▮ from it. This changes the pointer to a -¦- cross hair, and any existing links in the document become visible.

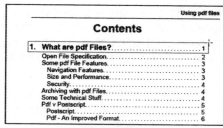

Fig. 10.24 Creating a Link

In Fig. 10.24 we are creating the first link from the Contents page of an eBook. You drag the -¦- pointer to create a marquee (rectangle) around the area 'hot spot' for the link. This is the area in which the link will be active when the book is being read. This opens the Create Link dialogue box, shown here in Fig. 10.25. We want a Web site type link that opens a page in the document, so choose the settings shown here. The **Link Type** should be Invisible Rectangle, and the **Link Action** should be **Go to a page view**. Click the **Help** button if you want to find out about the other types of links available. Clicking the **Next** button will set the link outline in red and open the Create Go to View message box. Ignore this box at the moment and navigate to the page in

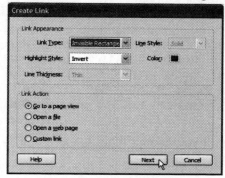

Fig. 10.25 The Create Link Box

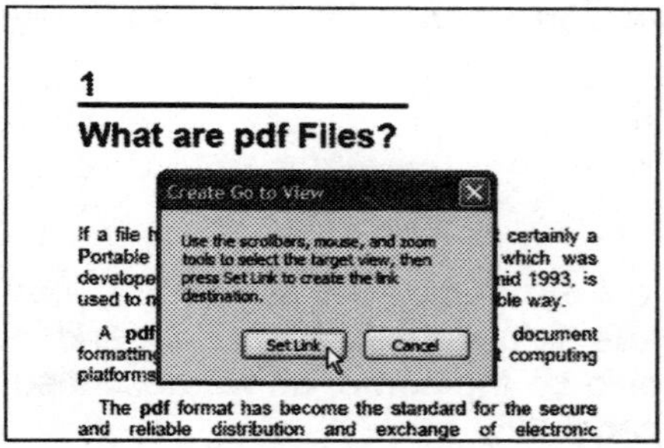

the document that you want to link to, as shown for us here in Fig. 10.26. Set the view size that you want and click **Set Link**. It takes five minutes to read about, but only five seconds to do!

Fig. 10.26 The Go to View

To test the link, select the Hand tool from the toolbar and move it over the new link area. The pointer should change shape from 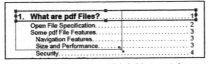 to , and clicking on the link should jump you to the new page. If not, something has gone wrong and it's time to try again.

1. What are pdf Files?.	1
Open File Specification.	2
Some pdf File Features.	3
Navigation Features.	3
Size and Performance.	3
Security.	4

Fig. 10.27 Resizing a Link Hotspot Area

You can edit a link at any time, to change its hotspot area or its action. To move or resize a link rectangle, select the Link tool and move the pointer over the link rectangle. The cross-hair -|- changes to an arrow ▶ when the pointer is moved over the link area, and red handles are placed around the border. To move the link rectangle, place the ▶ arrow anywhere in the rectangle, and drag it to the new location. To resize the link rectangle, drag any corner handle until the rectangle is the size you want, as shown in Fig. 10.27 above. To delete a link, select its rectangle with the Link tool and press the **Del** key.

That's enough on links. If you need it there is more detail in the Acrobat Help system.

The Finishing Touches

Before we finish this chapter on eBooks and the tools for creating them we must mention a few more things that may need attention.

Page Numbering

You will need to provide a clear numbering system for your eBook pages, and for Reader to use on the status bar and in the Pages tab. These should be the same, as we described in the section starting on page 135.

Headers and Footers

Headers and footers are text and numbers put at the top and bottom of your eBook pages. These can include book and chapter titles, page numbers and dates, etc. In **pdf** eBooks and documents there are two ways to place these.

You can place them in your source document with your word processor, and they will carry into the converted **pdf**. Using this method, you have more control over their formatting, but you can't edit them later in Acrobat.

Alternatively, you can create them in Acrobat. When done this way, you can easily delete or edit them in Acrobat, whenever you like. For details of this please look at page 137 in Chapter 8.

Including Metadata

As we saw on page 143, with Adobe Reader you can use the My Digital Editions window as a 'library' for your eBooks. For this to work properly you must embed some metadata into your **pdf** document in the Document Properties box.

To open this box, shown in Fig. 10.28 on the next page, you use the **File**, **Document Properties** command, or **Ctrl+D**.

Document metadata includes information about a document and its contents, and is also used by search engines. Some metadata is created automatically when a **pdf** file is created, as shown in the lower half of Fig. 10.28.

The top four text boxes of the Document Properties box let you manually add, the document title and subject, the author's name, and search keywords for the document. This you should always do, for obvious reasons.

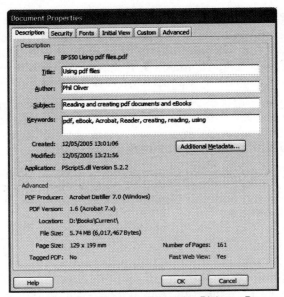

Fig. 10.28 The Document Properties Dialogue Box

Hopefully by now you have enough information to get started on preparing your own eBooks. Good luck and have fun doing it.

11

Adobe Acrobat Shortcuts

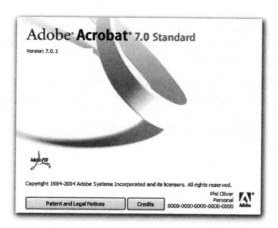

A keyboard shortcut is a function key, such as **F5**, or a key combination, such as **Ctrl+A**, that you use to carry out a menu command, or open a tool. An access key, on the other hand, is a key combination, such as **Alt+F**, that moves the focus to a menu, command, or control.

When we first started using computers, graphic interfaces like Windows and pointing tools like mice, had not been invented. The keyboard had to be used for everything, for entering data as well as the commands to manipulate it. Like most people in those days we became quite proficient with the keyboard. Times have changed. As Windows has improved as an operating system, pretty well all modern software is designed to be used graphically. You can now spend over half your time using a mouse to move you around a document and to find your way through menus and deep layers of dialogue boxes.

But if you watch a 'professional typist' he, or she, will still use the keyboard for most of the time. The majority of the programs regularly used today are built with a range of keyboard shortcuts. Touch typists find it much easier to learn and use these instead of taking their hands off the keyboard to pick up and play with a mouse.

In this chapter we explain the many keyboard shortcuts built into Adobe Acrobat 7, many require you to press two keys. For example, **Ctrl+A** means hold down the **Ctrl** key and press the letter **A**.

Before you can use all of the keyboard shortcuts in Acrobat, you must use the **Ctrl+K** shortcut to open the Preferences dialogue box, click the General link, select the **Use single-key accelerators to access tools** option and then press **OK**.

Menu Command Shortcuts

Many of Acrobat 7's keyboard shortcuts are listed on the program's main sub-menus.

File Menu

Ctrl+O	Open an existing **pdf** file.
Ctrl+N	Create a **pdf** from an existing file.
Shift+Ctrl+O	Create a **pdf** from a Web page.
Shift+Ctrl+1	Open the Organizer.
Shift+Ctrl+2	Add current file to a collection.
Ctrl+W	Close the current file.
Ctrl+S	Save the current file with the same name.
Shift+Ctrl+S	Save the current file with a new name.
Ctrl+D	Open the Document Properties box.
Ctrl+P	Open the Print dialogue box.
Shift+Ctrl+P	Set up the printer.
Ctrl+T	Print the document with comments.
Shift+Ctrl+9	Opens browser with PrintMe Web page.
Ctrl+Q	Exit the program.

Edit Menu

Ctrl+X	Cut selection to the clipboard.
Ctrl+C	Copy selection to the clipboard.
Ctrl+V	Paste clipboard contents.
Ctrl+Z	Undo the last command.
Shift+Ctrl+Z	Redo the last command.
Ctrl+A	Select all of the current page / document.
Shift+Ctrl+A	De-select all.
F7	Check spelling in comments / form fields.
Ctrl+B	Add a bookmark.
Ctrl+F	Open the Find toolbar.
Shift+Ctrl+F	Start a search operation.
Ctrl+]	Search next document.

Ctrl+[	Search previous document.
Ctrl+G	Next search result.
Shift+Ctrl+G	Previous search result.
Ctrl+K	Open the Preferences dialogue box.

View Menu

F4	Open or close the Navigation pane.
Ctrl+E	Open or close the Properties toolbar.
F8	Hide the toolbars.
Alt+ F8	Reset the toolbars.
Ctrl+F8	Dock all toolbars.
F9	Display or hide the main menu bar.
Ctrl+L	Go to full screen mode.
Ctrl+M	Open the Zoom To dialogue box.
Ctrl+1	Zoom to actual size.
Ctrl+0	Zoom to fit whole page in window.
Ctrl+2	Zoom to fit page width in window.
Ctrl+3	Zoom to fit margin width within window.
Ctrl+4	Reflow text.
Shift+Ctrl+H	Start or stop automatic scrolling of text.
Shift+Ctrl+V	Read current page out loud.
Shift+Ctrl+B	Read the rest of the document out loud.
Shift+Ctrl+C	Pause reading document out loud.
Shift+Ctrl+E	Stop reading out loud.
Home	Go to document first page.
⇒ / ⇐	Go to next / previous page.
End	Go to last page.
Shift+Ctrl+N	Go to a specific page number.
Alt+ ⇐	Go back to previous view.
Alt+ ⇒	Go to next view.
Alt+Shift+ ⇐	Go to previous document.
Alt+Shift+ ⇒	Go to next document.
Shift+Ctrl+Plus	Rotate view clockwise.
Shift+Ctrl+Minus	Rotate view anti-clockwise.

⇓	Scroll down.
Space	Scroll (when Hand tool is selected).
Ctrl+=	Zoom in.
Ctrl+hyphen	Zoom out.
Ctrl+Space	Zoom in temporarily.
Ctrl+Shift+Space	Zoom out temporarily.
Ctrl+M	Zoom to.

Working with Comments

S	**Note** tool.
E	**Text Edits** tool.
K	**Stamp** tool.
U	Current highlighting tool.
Shift+U	Cycle through highlighting tools: **Highlighter, Cross-Out Text** and **Underline Text**.
D	**Rectangle** tool.
Shift+D	Cycle through drawing tools: **Rectangle, Oval, Line, Polygon, Polygon Line**.
X	**Text Box** tool.
N	**Pencil** tool.
Shift+N	**Pencil Eraser** tool.
J	Attach file as a comment.
Shift+J	Cycle through attach tools: **Attach File, Attach Sound, Paste Clipboard Image**.
Tab	Move focus to comment.
F2	Move focus to text in comment.
Shift+Tab	Move focus to next comment.
Space	Open pop-up window for comment.
O	Send and receive comments.
Y	Save document and work off-line, in a browser-based review.
I	Go back on-line.

General Navigation

F9	Show/hide menu bar.
F10	Move focus to menus.
Shift+F8	Move focus to toolbar in browser.
Ctrl+E	Open Properties toolbar.
Ctrl+I	Open Properties dialogue box.
Ctrl+F6	Cycle through open documents (focus in document pane).
Ctrl+Shift+F6	Cycle backwards through open documents (focus in document pane).
Ctrl+F4	Close current document.
Ctrl+Shift+W	Close all windows.
F5	Move focus to document pane.
Shift+F5	Move focus to status bar when it is in the document pane.
F6	Move focus to next pane or panel.
Shift+F6	Move focus to previous pane or panel.
Tab	Move focus to next comment, link or form field in the document pane.
Shift+Tab	Move focus to previous comment, link or form field in the document pane.
Space or Enter	Activate selected tool, item (such as a movie or bookmark), or command.
Shift+F10	Open/ context menu.
F10	Close context menu.
Esc	Return to Hand tool.
Ctrl+Tab	Move focus to next tab in a tabbed dialogue box.
F3	Move to next search result.
Shift+arrow keys	Select text (when **Select Text** tool is active).
Ctrl+ ⇒/⇐	Move cursor to next/previous word (when **Select Text** tool is active).

Working with Navigation Tabs

F4	Open/close navigation pane.
Ctrl+Shift+F5	Open and move focus to navigation pane.
F6	Move focus between the areas of a document.
Tab	Move focus to next element of the active navigation tab: Trash Can, Options menu, Close box, tab contents, and tab.
⇑ or ⇓	Move to next navigation tab and make it active (when focus is on the tab).
Ctrl+Tab	Move to next navigation tab and make it active (focus anywhere in the navigation pane).
⇒ or Shift+plus	Expand the current bookmark (when focus is on the Bookmarks tab).
⇐ or minus	Collapse the current bookmark (when focus is on the Bookmarks tab).
Shift+*	Expand all bookmarks.
/	Collapse selected bookmark.
⇓	Move focus to next item in a navigation tab.
⇑	Move focus to previous item in a navigation tab.

The Help Window

F1	Open/close Help window.
Ctrl+W or Alt+F4	Close Help window.
Shift+F8	Move focus to toolbar in Help window.
⇑ or ⇓	Move to next element in active tab.
⇒ or ⇐	Move focus among tabs: Contents, Search, Index.
Tab	Toggle focus between active tab and tab contents.

The How To Pane

Shift+F4	Open/close the How To pane.
Shift+F1	Open and move focus to How To pane.
Home	Go to How To home page.
Ctrl+Tab	Move focus among the elements of the How To pane.
Tab	Move focus down through the elements of the How To pane.
Shift+Tab	Move focus up through the elements of the How To pane.
⇒	Go to next page in How To pane.
⇐	Go to previous page in How To pane.

Keys for Editing

Ctrl+A	Select all content.
Ctrl+Shift+A	Deselect all content.
Ctrl+9	Browse for a folder.
Ctrl+0	Fit page.
Shift+F5	Move focus to status tray.

Scrolling Automatically

The automatic scrolling feature, activated with the **View**, **Automatically Scroll** menu command or **Shift+Ctrl+H**, makes it easier to scan through a long document. In this mode you can use the following keyboard shortcuts:

0 to 9, or ⇧/⇩	Change the scrolling speed, where 9 is the fastest and 0 is the slowest.
—	Reverse the direction of the scrolling.
⇐ or ⇒	Jump to the next or previous page.
Esc	Stop automatic scrolling.

12

Glossary of Terms

Acrobat Distiller	A program used for converting documents to PostScript language files.
Actions	Processes used to extend the functionality of a document; a wide range of actions are available, such as printing, opening other programs or documents, or viewing snapshots.
Active	Describes the folder, window or icon that you are currently using or that is currently selected.
Add-in	A mini-program which runs in conjunction with another and enhances its functionality.
Address	A unique number or name that identifies a specific computer or user on a network.
Administrator	For Windows XP Professional, a person responsible for setting up and managing local computers, their user and group accounts, and assigning passwords and permissions.
Adobe Reader	The latest version of Adobe's **pdf** Reader, Adobe Reader 7.0 replaces earlier versions of Acrobat Reader as well as the Adobe eBook Reader.
Anonymous FTP	Anonymous FTP allows you to connect to a remote computer and transfer public files back to your local

computer without the need to have a user ID and password.

Anti-aliasing

Smoothing of jagged edges in images by combining the colours of the foreground pixels with the background pixels at the edges of an image.

Applet

A program that can be downloaded over a network and launched on the user's computer.

Application

Software (program) designed to carry out a certain activity, such as word processing, or data management.

Application alert

A pop-up message that displays when executing program commands. Alerts include information, warning, caution, and error messages.

Article box

An area of a page defined by the Article tool. An Article box is not linked to the page content in any way; it can be resized or repositioned anywhere on a page.

Article thread

A sequence of numbered Article boxes read in order of their numbering rather than location on a document.

Articles

A method to control the reading order in a document by defining page segments and sequences.

ASCII

A binary code representation of a character set. The name stands for 'American Standard Code for Information Interchange'.

Association

An identification of a filename extension to a program. This lets

Windows open the program when its files are selected.

Audio input device

A device that records music and voice input into your computer, such as a microphone or a CD-ROM player.

Authentication

The process for verifying that an entity or object is who or what it claims to be.

Authoring

The process of creating Web documents or software.

Automatic scrolling

An option to move a document vertically through the Document pane without using keystrokes or mouse clicks.

Background

The screen background image used on a graphical user interface such as Windows.

Backup

To make a back-up copy of a file or a disc for safekeeping. Make a secondary copy of an eBook in case the primary copy is damaged or corrupted.

Bandwidth

The range of transmission frequencies a network can use. The greater the bandwidth the more information that can be transferred over a network.

Banner

An advertising graphic shown on a Web page.

Baseline offset

The line where text sits above or below the baseline, the line on which the text is drawn.

BASIC	Beginner's All-purpose Symbolic Instruction Code - a high-level programming language.
Basic volume	A primary partition or logical drive that resides on a basic disc.
Baud rate	The speed at which a modem communicates.
Beta test	A test of software that is still under development, by people actually using the software.
Binary	A base-2 number system in which values are expressed as combinations of two digits, 0 and 1.
Binder	A collection of documents combined into one **pdf** document.
BIOS	On x86-based computers, the set of software routines that test hardware at startup, start the operating system, and support the transfer of data among hardware devices.
Bit	The smallest unit of information handled by a computer.
Bitmap	A technique for managing the image displayed on a computer screen.
Bookmark destination	The view displayed in the Document pane when a bookmark is clicked in the Bookmarks panel.
Bookmark	An identified location in a document. A bookmark is a type of link from text on the Bookmarks tab in the Navigation pane to a different view or page in the document.

Bounding box	The area defined when a selection tool is used to select an object, portion of a page, or image.
Boot up	To start your computer by switching it on, which initiates a self test of its Random Access Memory (RAM), then loads the necessary system files.
Broadband	A communications systems in which the medium of transmission (such as a wire or fibre-optic cable) carries multiple messages at a time.
Broadcast	An address that is destined for all hosts on a particular network segment.
Browse	A button in some Windows dialogue boxes that lets you view a list of files and folders before you make a selection.
Browser	A program, like Internet Explorer, that lets you view Web pages.
Bug	An error in coding or logic that causes a program to malfunction.
Bus	A communication line used for data transfer among the components of a computer system.
Button	A graphic element in a dialogue box or toolbar that performs a specified function.
Byte	A unit of data that holds a single character, such as a letter, a digit.
Cache	An area of memory, or disc space, reserved for data, which speeds up downloading.

Capture	The process of analysing an image of a document and converting it to text characters.
CCITT Gp 3 and 4	Image compression methods developed and supported by the International Coordinating Committee for Telephony and Telegraphy. Compression used for black and white images made by paint programs and scans. Group 3 and Group 4 refer to specific compression methods.
Card	A removable printed-circuit board that is plugged into a computer expansion slot.
CD-R	Recordable compact disc.
CD-ROM	Read Only Memory compact disc. Data can be read but not written.
CD-RW	Rewritable compact disc. Data can be copied to the CD on more than one occasion and can be erased.
Certificate	A file containing information about a digital signature as well as its encryption numbers.
Certification	A method of securing a document used by the document author. A certified document is signed using a digital signature; its content is restricted to a user list, and its actions are restricted according to settings chosen on certification.
Character spacing	Adding space between characters in selected text.
Click	To press and release a mouse button once without moving the mouse.

Client	A computer that has access to services over a computer network. The computer providing the services is a server.
Client application	A Windows application that can accept linked, or embedded, objects.
Clipboard	A temporary storage area of memory, where text and graphics are stored with the Windows cut and copy actions.
Cluster	In data storage, the smallest amount of disc space that can be allocated to hold a file.
CMYK	Abbreviation for cyan, magenta, yellow, and black; the inks used in process printing. They represent the subtractive colour model, where a combination of 100% of each component yields black and 0% of each yields white.
Code page	A means of providing support for character sets and keyboard layouts for different countries or regions.
Colour space	A portion of a colour model with a specific range of colours. For example, within the RGB colour model are a number of colour spaces like Adobe RGB, sRGB, and so on.
Command	An instruction given to a computer to carry out a particular action.
Comments list	The horizontal display of a document's comments shown below the document in the program window.
Comments	Information added to a document using a number of tools such as

	notes, drawn lines, recorded sound, and so on.
Compatibility Level	Settings chosen for different functions such as security and printing that are available in different versions of Acrobat.
Complete Help	The help files for Reader or Acrobat program. The complete help files contains information about using the program.
Compressed file	One that is compacted to save server space and reduce transfer times. Typical file extensions for compressed files include .zip (DOS/Windows) and .tar (UNIX).
Compression	A file processing method used to decrease the size of **pdf** image files; using the correct format decreases the file size without affecting the quality of the file.
Configuration	A general purpose term referring to the way you have your computer set up.
Contents (Help)	A nested display of the Help file's contents; the default view when the Acrobat Complete Help Files are opened.
Controls	Objects on a form, report, or data access page that display data, perform actions, or are used for decoration.
Conversion	The process of reading a source document's code and structure and writing the **pdf** equivalent.

Cookies	Files stored on your hard drive by your Web browser that hold information for it to use.
Corrupt signature	A digital signature that cannot be compared to the digital certificate on your computer.
CPU	The Central Processing Unit; the main chip that executes all instructions entered into a computer.
Cropping	Removing segments of the edges of a document. Use the Crop dialogue box in Acrobat to revise page size by cropping areas from all sides of the document.
Cross-platform files	Media and other files that work on both Windows and Mac operating systems.
CSV	Comma Separated Values. A structure used for defining content location in a spreadsheet. Each cell value is separated by a comma. Tables exported from Acrobat use CSV format export.
CSV-compliant	A program that is capable of reading data using a comma separated value format.
Cyberspace	Originated by William Gibson in his novel 'Neuromancer', now used to describe the Internet and the other computer networks.
Data access page	A Web page, created by Access, that has a connection to a database; you can view, add, edit, and manipulate the data in this page.

Data packet	A unit of information transmitted as a whole from one device to another on a network.
Database	A collection of data related to a particular topic or purpose.
DBMS	Database management system - A software interface between the database and the user.
Default	The command, device or option automatically chosen.
Defragmentation	The process of rewriting parts of a file to contiguous sectors on a hard disc to increase the speed of access and retrieval.
Desktop	The Windows screen working background, on which you place icons, folders, etc.
Destination	A method of linking documents where a location is named in one document and then linked using a bookmark or link from another document.
Device driver	A special file that must be loaded into memory for Windows to be able to address a specific procedure or hardware device.
Device name	A logical name used by DOS to identify a device, such as LPT1 or COM1 for the parallel or serial printer.
Dial-up connection	The connection to a network via a device that uses the telephone network. This includes modems with a standard phone line, ISDN cards with high-speed ISDN lines, or X.25 networks.

Dialogue box	A window displayed on the screen to allow the user to enter information.
Digital signature	A method of defining a unique signature for a person used to attach to digital documents. Signatures are used to certify content in a number of ways such as complete, unaltered, or reviewed. Also know as a profile or digital ID.
Direct connection	A permanent connection between your computer system and the Internet.
Directory	An area on disc where information relating to a group of files is kept. Also known as a folder.
Disconnect	To detach a drive, port or computer from a shared device, or to break an Internet connection.
Display adapter	An expansion board that plugs into a PC to give it display capabilities.
Distiller driver	A printer driver used to convert source documents to **pdf**.
Distribute	Method to set the location of a group of selected links (minimum of three) on a page. Distributed links are spaced evenly horizontally or vertically.
DLL	Dynamic Link Library; An OS feature that allows files with the .dll extensions to be loaded only when needed by the program.
Docked Toolbar	A toolbar that is situated with other toolbars at the top of the program window under the main menu

	headings or at the far left or far right of the program window.
Document	A file produced by an application program.
Document pane	The portion of the program window that displays the open document.
Document properties	Information about a document, including its size, keywords, creation time and authoring program. Document properties may be added in some source programs, or in Acrobat.
Document status	Items attached to a document such as security, signatures, or layers, displayed at the bottom of the Reader window in the status bar.
Document trust level	A preference setting used for individual documents.
Domain	A group of devices, servers and computers on a network.
Domain name	The name of an Internet site, for example www.philoliver.com. These allow you to reference Internet sites without knowing their true numerical address.
DOS	Disc Operating System. A collection of small specialised programs that allow interaction between user and computer.
Double-click	To quickly press and release a mouse button twice.
Download	To transfer to your computer a file, or data, from another computer.

Downsampling	Combining pixels in a sample area to make a larger pixel, resulting in a smaller file size. In Acrobat, pixels in images with a resolution above a specified amount are combined to reduce the resolution.
DPI	Dots Per Inch - a resolution standard for laser printers.
Drag	To move an object on the screen by pressing and holding down the left mouse button while moving the mouse.
Drive name	The letter followed by a colon which identifies a floppy or hard disc drive.
DRM	Digital Rights Management. A process of controlling access to eBooks and other electronic media. DRM uses different methods to control the purchase, download, and security of electronic media.
DSL	Digital Subscriber Line - a broadband connection to the Internet through existing copper telephone wires.
DVD	Digital Video Disc; a type of optical disc technology. It looks like a CD but can store greater amounts of data.
Dynamic stamp	Image stamps that include the user name, date, and time the stamp was applied to the document.
eBook categories	Labels used to sort eBooks by type. Acrobat includes a set of default categories.
eBook	A **pdf** document designed to be read on a screen as a book.

ECard	A personal greeting card sent via e-mail or CD; eCards created in Photoshop Album can be used in Acrobat.
E-mail	Electronic Mail - A system that allows computer users to send and receive messages electronically.
Embedded object	Information in a document that is 'copied' from its source application. Selecting the object opens the creating application from within the document.
Embedding	Information about fonts in a document is automatically attached for use after the document is converted to **pdf**.
Encrypted password	A password that is scrambled.
Encryption	A software-based method of controlling who has access to a document. Encryption is described in levels; the higher the level of encryption, the greater level of control you have over the document and actions related to the document.
Engine	Software used by search services.
eps	Encapsulated PostScript - The graphics file format used by the PostScript language.
Ethernet	A very common method of networking computers in a LAN.
Expansion slot	A socket in a computer, designed to hold expansion boards and connect them to the system bus.

Extract

Extracting removes a page or page range from a document.

FAQ

Frequently Asked Questions - A common feature on the Internet, FAQs are files of answers to commonly asked questions.

Fast Web View

A setting that allows a **pdf** document to be downloaded one page at a time from a server.

FAT

The File Allocation Table. An area on disc where information is kept on which part of the disc a file is located.

File extension

The suffix following the period in a filename. Windows uses this to identify the source application program. For example .mdb indicates an Access file.

Filename

The name given to a file. In Windows 95 and above this can be up to 256 characters long.

Filter

A set of criteria that is applied to data to show a subset of the data.

Firewall

Security measures designed to protect a networked system from unauthorised access.

Flash

Multimedia technology developed by Macromedia to allow interactive elements to documents and Web sites, or for creating entire Flash sites. Flash files have the .swf format.

Flattened layer

A document imported from Visio or AutoCAD can use multiple layers added by the document author. Flattened layers compress content from the original document into one single layer.

Floating toolbar
An open toolbar that is not docked at the top or sides of the program window. (Undocked toolbar).

Floppy disc
A removable disc on which information can be stored magnetically.

Folder
An area used to store a group of files, usually with a common link.

Font
A graphic design representing a set of characters, numbers and symbols.

Format
The structure of a file that defines the way it is stored and laid out on the screen or in print.

Fragmentation
The scattering of parts of the same file over different areas of the disc.

Free space
Available disc space that can be used to create logical drives within an extended partition.

Freeware
Software that is available for downloading and unlimited use without charge.

FTP
File Transfer Protocol. The procedure for connecting to a remote computer and transferring files.

FTP Address
File Transfer Protocol address; a location of a Web server used to transfer files.

Full Screen View
An Acrobat and Reader viewing and opening option that displays the document using the full screen.

Function key	One of the series of 10 or 12 keys marked with the letter F and a numeral, used for specific operations.
Gateway	A computer system that allows otherwise incompatible networks to communicate with each other.
GIF	Graphics Interchange Format, a common standard for images on the Web.
Gigabyte	(GB); 1,024 megabytes. Usually thought of as one billion bytes.
Gradient	An image that is coloured in varying numbers of colours and uses a smooth transition between one colour and another.
Graphic	A picture or illustration, also called an image. Formats include GIF, JPEG, BMP, PCX, and TIFF.
Graphics card	A device that controls the display on the monitor and other allied functions.
Grayscale	An image coloured in shades of grey. Continuous-tone images, such as black-and-white photographs, use an almost unlimited number of shades of grey.
Greek Text	An option to display very small text as grey lines rather than individual letters, decreasing the length of time it takes to display the document content on the screen.
Group	A collection of users, computers, contacts, and other groups.
GUI	A Graphic User Interface, such as Windows, the software front-end

	meant to provide an attractive and easy to use interface.
Handshaking	A series of signals acknowledging that communication can take place between computers or other devices.
Hard copy	Output on paper.
Hard disc	A device built into the computer for holding programs and data.
Hardware	The equipment that makes up a computer system, excluding the programs or software.
Headers and Footers	Text and images such as a logo, page number, or date that display at the top and bottom of specified pages in a document.
Help	A Windows system that gives you instructions and additional information on using a program.
Hibernation	A state in which your computer shuts down after saving everything in memory onto your hard disc.
Hierarchy	A structure for organising content. Bookmarks and tags are both nested in hierarchies.
High Quality	Distiller Job Option - A collection of conversion settings used for high-quality output; prints to a higher image resolution but doesn't embed font information. High quality sets the printing resolution to 2,400 dpi.
Home page	The document displayed when you first open your Web browser, or the first document you come to at a Web site.

Horizontal scaling	The proportion between the height and the width of type; scaling can be adjusted to more or less than 100%, with 100% as the default scale for the font.
Host	Computer connected directly to the Internet that provides services to other local and/or remote computers.
How To?	A pane displayed at the right of the program window displaying a set of links to common functions and tasks.
HTML	HyperText Markup Language, the original format used in documents on the Web.
HTML editor	Authoring tool which assists with the creation of HTML pages.
HTTP	HyperText Transport Protocol, the system used to link and transfer hypertext documents on the Web.
Hub	A common connection point for devices in a network.
Hyperlink	A segment of text, or an image, that refers to another document on the Web, an intranet or your PC.
Hypermedia	Hypertext extended to include linked multimedia.
Hypertext	A system that allows documents to be cross-linked so that the reader can explore related links, or documents, by clicking on a highlighted symbol.
Icon	A small graphic image that represents a function or object. Clicking an icon produces an action.

Image	See graphic.
Image Viewer Plug-In	A program plug-in that is activated when a Photoshop Album product such as a presentation is opened in Acrobat.
Index (Help)	An alphabetical listing of the contents of the Complete Acrobat Help Files.
Index	A searchable database of the content of a document or set of documents. An index can be searched in Acrobat Standard; index creation is only available in Acrobat Professional.
Info panel	A Navigation panel displaying the x and y co-ordinates of the cursor's location on a page.
Initial View	The view presented to the user when a **pdf** document is opened. Set by the user or by the document author.
Insert	Inserting adds a specified page or pages from one **pdf** to a target **pdf**.
Insertion point	A flashing bar that shows where typed text will be entered into a document.
Interface	A device that allows you to connect a computer to its peripherals.
Internet	The global system of computer networks.
Intranet	A private network inside an organisation using the same kind of software as the Internet.
IP	Internet Protocol - The rules that provide basic Internet functions.

IP Address	Internet Protocol Address - every computer on the Internet has a unique identifying number.
ISA	Industry Standard Architecture; a standard for internal PC connections.
ISDN	Integrated Services Digital Network; a telecom standard using digital transmission technology to support voice, video and data communications applications over regular telephone lines.
ISP	Internet Service Provider - A company that offers access to the Internet.
Java	An object-oriented programming language created by Sun Microsystems for developing applications and applets that are capable of running on any computer, regardless of the operating system.
JavaScript	A scripting language used for constructing many Acrobat processes.
Job options	Groups of Distiller conversion settings used to convert a source document to a **pdf** document. The program includes a set of four default job options, Standard, High Quality, Press Quality, and Smallest File Size.
JPEG / JPG	Joint Photographic Experts Group, a popular cross-platform format for image files. JPEG is best suited for true colour original images.
Kernel	The core of layered architecture that manages the most basic operations

of the operating system and the computer's processor.

Key

A string of numbers generated by an encryption algorithm.

Keyboard navigation

Moving through a document and its commands using keystrokes instead of mouse clicks.

Keyboard shortcut

A key, or keys, that you use to carry out a menu command, or open a tool.

Kilobyte

(KB); 1024 bytes of information or storage space.

LAN

Local Area Network - High-speed, privately-owned network covering a limited geographical area, such as an office or a building.

Laptop

A portable computer small enough to sit on your lap.

Layer visibility

In a layered document, content layers can be visible or invisible depending on the author's settings. Visible layers are seen in the Document pane.

Layers

Document levels displaying different content. In a regular **pdf** document, the background contains only a colour or an applied image, the text and image content sits on the document layer. Comments, link, bookmarks, and other actions sit on a layer above the document layer.

LCD

Liquid Crystal Display.

Linked object

An object that is inserted into a document but still exists in the source file. Changing the original object automatically updates it within the linked document.

Link

Text or a graphic used to connect information or activity from one place in a document to information or activity in another location in the same or another document. Also a hypertext connection between Web pages.

Linux

A version of the UNIX operating system for PCs which incorporates a Graphical User Interface (GUI) similar to that of Microsoft Windows.

Local

A resource that is located on your computer, not linked to it over a network.

Location

An Internet address.

Locked font

A font whose licence doesn't allow embedding in a document.

Logical order

The numbering method used in a document. Pages are numbered according to their location in a document. Logical order numbers appear on the status bar of the program along with added page numbers.

Log on

To gain access to a network.

Make accessible

The Acrobat command that adds tags to a document.

Marquee

The hatched lines that appear on a document page as you drag the pointer with a selection tool, such as the Snapshot tool. When the mouse is released, the content within the hatched rectangle is selected.

MCI	Media Control Interface - a standard for files and multimedia devices.
Megabyte	(MB); 1024 kilobytes of information or storage space.
Megahertz	(MHz); Speed of processor in millions of cycles per second.
Memory	Part of a computer consisting of storage elements organised into addressable locations that can hold data and instructions.
Menu	A list of available options in an application.
MIDI	Musical Instrument Digital Interface - enables devices to transmit and receive sound and music messages.
MIME	Multipurpose Internet Mail Extensions, a messaging standard that allows Internet users to exchange e-mails enhanced with graphics, video and voice.
MIPS	Million Instructions Per Second; measures speed of a system.
Modem	Short for Modulator-demodulator. An electronic device that lets computers communicate electronically.
Monitor	The display device connected to your PC, also called a screen.
Mouse	A device used to manipulate a pointer around your display and activate processes by pressing buttons.
MPEG	Motion Picture Experts Group - a video file format offering excellent quality in a relatively small file.

MS-DOS	Microsoft's implementation of the Disc Operating System for PCs.
Multimedia	The use of photographs, music and sound and movie images in a presentation.
Multitasking	Performing more than one operation at the same time.
My Documents	A folder on your hard disc that provides a convenient place to store documents, graphics, or other files you want to access quickly.
Navigation pane	A set of tabs displayed down the left side of the Acrobat or Reader window. Collectively the tabs are referred to as the Navigation Pane.
Nesting	A way of organising information in a hierarchy.
Network	Two or more computers connected together to share resources.
Network adapter	A device that connects your computer to a network.
Network server	Central computer which stores files for several linked computers.
Node	Any single computer connected to a network.
NTFS file system	An advanced file system that provides performance, security, reliability, and advanced features that are not found in any version of FAT.
OCR	Optical Character Recognition. A process where bitmap representations of characters are analysed and converted to the equivalent text characters.

OLE	Object Linking and Embedding - A technology for transferring and sharing information among software applications.
Online	Having access to the Internet.
On-line Service	Services such as America On-line and CompuServe that provide content to subscribers and usually connections to the Internet.
Opacity	The level at which an object covers an underlying object on a page. An opacity level of 100% means underlying layers are completely hidden. Adjust opacity levels for watermarks and backgrounds.
Operating system	Software that runs a computer.
Overprinting	Colours in a colour print that are printed on top of each other. In the CMYK colour system, cyan is printed over magenta, which is printed over yellow, which is printed over black.
Page cache	A buffer area used to store pages. As you display one page the next page in a document is read and placed in a buffer area until you are ready to view it, speeding up page loading time.
Page layout	Options for viewing pages in Acrobat. Pages can be viewed as single pages, as a continuous scroll, or in facing views. You select the page layout in the status bar at the bottom of the program window.
Parallel port	The input/output connector for a parallel interface device. Printers are generally plugged into a parallel port.

Partition	A portion of a physical disc that functions as though it were a physically separate disc.
Password	A unique character string used to gain access to a network, program, or mailbox.
PATH	The location of a file in the directory tree.
PCI	Peripheral Component Interconnect - a type of slot in your computer which accepts similar type peripheral cards.
pdf	Portable Data Format, the format used in Adobe Acrobat.
PDFMaker	A macro and toolbar added to Microsoft Office products when Acrobat is installed. Used to generate **pdf** documents from the program.
Peripheral	Any device attached to a PC.
Perl	A popular language for programming CGI applications.
Photoshop Album	An Adobe product used to manage images and create specific products such as presentations and eCards. Content from Photoshop Album can be used in Acrobat.
Picture Tasks plug-in	A set of commands that display in Acrobat when a Photoshop Album product such as a presentation is opened in Acrobat.
PIF file	Program information file - gives information to Windows about an MS-DOS application.
Pixel	A picture element on screen; the smallest element that can be

	independently assigned colour and intensity.
Player	A program that is either part of an operating system or a plug-in, used for playing different types of audio and video media.
Plug-and-play	Hardware which can be plugged into a PC and be used immediately without configuration.
POP	Post Office Protocol - a method of storing and returning e-mail.
Port	The place where information goes into or out of a computer, e.g. a modem might be connected to the serial port.
PostScript	A page-description language (PDL), developed by Adobe Systems for printing on laser printers.
PPK Encryption	A method of document encryption where each person has both a public key shared with others as well as a private key used to access secure documents on their computer.
Press Quality	Distiller Job Option - A collection of conversion settings used for high-end print production, such as image setters. All the information possible is added to the file. This setting requires font embedding, and prints at a high resolution.
Print queue	A list of print jobs waiting to be sent to a printer.
Profile	A method of defining a unique signature for a person used to attach

	to digital documents. Also know as a digital signature or digital ID.
Program	A set of instructions which cause a computer to perform tasks.
Properties bar	A dynamic Acrobat toolbar. Its contents change depending on the tool and document content selected.
Protocol	A set of rules or standards that define how computers communicate with each other.
Queue	A list of e-mail messages waiting to be sent over the Internet.
QuickTime	A media player that plays .mov files.
RAM	Random Access Memory. The computer's volatile memory. Data held in it is lost when power is switched off.
RC4 Encryption	Technology developed by RSA Data Security, Inc. to control access to a document.
Read out loud	An Adobe option to read the contents of a document aloud. You can choose from several different voices and adjust other characteristics such as volume and speed.
Real mode	MS-DOS mode, typically used to run programs, such as MS-DOS games, that will not run under Windows.
Recipient list	A list of users specified to be able to open and work with a document.
Refresh	To update displayed information with current data.
Registered file type	File types that are tracked by the system registry and are recognised

	by the programs you have installed on your computer.
Registry	A database where information about a computer's configuration is deposited. The registry contains information that Windows continually references during its operation.
Remote computer	A computer that you can access only by using a communications line or a communications device, such as a network card or a modem.
Replace	Replacing pages in Acrobat removes the page layer from a specified page or pages in a document and replaces them with the page layer from another document.
Resolution	The number of pixels per image, which affects the crispness of detail or fineness of grain. Screen resolution is measured in dots by lines, such as 800x600; printer resolution is measured in dpi, such as 600 dpi.
Resource	A directory, or printer, that can be shared over a network.
Revert	A command used to restore the document to its last saved form.
Review Cycle	A method of sharing documents with a group of people.
RGB	Abbreviation for red, green, blue; the colours used on monitors. They represents the additive colour model, where 0% of each component yields black and 100% of each component yields white.

Robot	A Web agent that visits sites for the purpose of indexing for search engines. Also known as Wanderers, Crawlers, or Spiders.
ROM	Read Only Memory. A PC's non-volatile memory. Data is written into this memory at manufacture and is not affected by power loss.
Root	The highest or uppermost level in a hierarchic disc directory.
Rotation	Changing the orientation of a document page.
RSA Algorithm	A mathematical string used as an encryption standard especially for data transmitted by Internet methods.
Run Length	A compression method used for images with large areas of solid black or white.
Scanning	The process of converting printed material to digital format using a scanner.
Screen saver	A moving picture or pattern that appears on your screen when you have not used the mouse or keyboard for a specified time.
Script	A type of program consisting of a set of instructions to an application or tool program.
Scroll bar	A bar that appears at the right side or bottom edge of a window.
Search	Submit a query to a search engine.
Search engine	A program that helps users find information across the Internet.

Search (Help)	An option for displaying Help File content; type a search term and click Search to display a list of topics containing the search term.
Secure Document	Protecting the content and manipulation of a document using passwords or signatures.
Self-sign Security	A method used for securing **pdf** documents using signatures you manage, control, and share.
Serial interface	An interface that transfers data as individual bits.
Server	A computer system that manages and delivers information for client computers.
Shared resource	Any device, program or file that is available to network users.
Shareware	Software that is available on public networks and bulletin boards. Users are expected to pay a nominal amount to the software developer.
Shortcut	A link to any item accessible from your computer.
Signature field	A field added to a **pdf** document used for holding a digital signature. The field may be visible or invisible.
Signature file	An ASCII text file, maintained within e-mail programs, that contains text for your signature.
Site	A place on the Internet containing Web pages.
Smallest File Size	Distiller Job Option - A collection of conversion settings used to create the smallest file size possible; used

for distributing content for the Web, e-mail, or onscreen viewing. Images are compressed and downsampled.

Snapshot	A tool used to capture a specified portion of a page. The captured image is copied to the clipboard.
Software	The programs and instructions that control your PC.
Sort	A method of displaying content in some program panels according to specified characteristics.
Source document	The document or file created in a program that is converted to **pdf** for use in Acrobat or Adobe Reader.
Source program	A computer program used to generate documents that can be converted to **pdf** documents.
Spamming	Sending the same message to a large number of mailing lists or newsgroups.
Splash screen	An opening screen showing the program name, logo and version.
Stamps	A collection of commenting tools used to add common business messages to a page.
Standard	Distiller Job Option - A collection of conversion settings used for basic business document conversion and viewing. Standard settings use a printing resolution of 600 dpi.
Standby	A state in which your computer consumes less power when it is idle, but remains available for use.

Status bar	The horizontal bar below the Document pane that displays page numbers, viewing layout, page navigation options, and special icons such as Layers or Certification.
Stroke width	Width of a line outlining a text character.
Structure elements	A list of the tags in a document accessible from the Bookmarks menu when using a tagged document.
Styles	A set of formatting characteristics applied to text, tables, and lists in a document. Acrobat bookmarks can be built based on styles used in Microsoft Word documents.
Submit	A forms process where the content of a form's fields or the form itself are transmitted via e-mail, to a Web server, or stored in a file.
Subscribe	To become a member of.
Subsetting	A percentage of an embedded font's information based on the number of characters used in the document.
Surfing	The process of looking around the Internet.
Suspects	In an OCR process, the characters the program was unable to definitively convert.
System files	Files used by Windows to load, configure, and run the operating system.
Tagged bookmarks	A bookmark structure based on the tagged structure of a document.

Tagging	The process of creating a logical structure for a document, and defining relationships among elements in the document, including tables, lists, images, and text. Tags can be added in some source programs, as well as within Acrobat.
Task buttons	A set of icons that display commands related to functional processes, such as Digital Signatures and Comments.
Task Manager	A utility that provides information about programs and processes running on the computer. Using Task Manager, you can end or run programs and end processes, and display a dynamic overview of your computer's performance.
Text attributes	Characteristics of a font including the size, fill, stroke, embedding, subsetting, spacing, baseline.
Text Edit Tools	A group of commenting tools designed specifically to markup a document and export to Word for integration into the original Word document.
Text file	An unformatted file of text characters saved in ASCII format.
Text link	A link created by drawing a link box over text on a document page.
Thumbnail	A miniature representation of a document page or an image. In Acrobat, page thumbnails are displayed in the Pages panel and can be used to manipulate the content of the document.

Toggle	To turn an action on and off with the same switch.
Toolbar	A bar containing icons giving quick access to commands.
Tooltips	Boxes that display when the pointer is held over a tool or icon.
Touchup Text	An editing function in Acrobat that lets you select and modify text in a document or add lines of text.
Tracking	Controlling the location of a review process. You can see the status of a review, such as recipient lists using the Review Tracker.
Transition	Visual effects applied when one page replaces another, such as wipes and dissolves.
TrueType fonts	Fonts that can be scaled to any size and print as they show on the screen.
Undocked toolbar	An open toolbar that is not docked at the top or sides of the program window.
Uninstall	When referring to software, the act of removing program files and folders from your hard disc and removing related data from your registry.
UNIX	Multitasking, multi-user computer operating system that is run by many computer servers on networks.
Upload/Download	The process of transferring files between computers. Files are uploaded from your computer to another and downloaded from another computer to your own.

URL	Uniform Resource Locator, the addressing system used on the Web, containing information about the method of access, the server to be accessed and the path of the file to be accessed.
USB	Universal Serial Bus - an external bus standard that enables data transfer rates of 12 Mbps.
Usenet	Informal network of computers that allow the posting and reading of messages in newsgroups.
User ID	The unique identifier, usually used in conjunction with a password, which identifies you on a computer.
User list	A list of contacts allowed to view content of a protected document.
User password	A password added to a document to prevent unauthorised viewing of the document.
View	The document location, page, and magnification displayed when a bookmark or destination link is clicked.
Virus	A malicious program, downloaded from a web site or disc, designed to wipe out information on your computer.
Watermarks	Repeating elements that overlay the page content in a document such as 'Draft' or 'Confidential'.
Web	A network of hypertext-based multimedia information servers. Browsers are used to view any information on the Web.

Web page	An document that is accessible on the Web.
Wizard	A Microsoft tool that asks you questions and then creates an object depending on your answers.
Word spacing	Adding space between words in selected text.
XHTML	Extensible Hypertext Markup Language, a hybrid between HTML and XML.
XML	eXtensible Markup Language. A file format that defines a document's structure. Converting data to XML creates data that can be read by many different types of applications.
ZIP compression	A compression method suitable for compressing images with large areas of single colour or repeating patterns.
Zoom	The magnification view of the document.

Index

Companion Discs

COMPANION DISCS are available for some of the computer books written by the same author(s) and published by BERNARD BABANI (publishing) LTD, as listed at the front of this book (except for those marked with an asterisk).

There is no Companion Disc for this book

To obtain companion discs for other books, fill in the order form below, or a copy of it, enclose a cheque (payable to **P.R.M. Oliver**) or a postal order, and send it to the address given below. **Make sure you fill in your name and address** and specify the book number and title in your order.

Book No.	Book Name	Unit Price	Total Price
BP		£3.50	
BP		£3.50	
BP		£3.50	
Name		Sub-total	£............
Address		P & P (@ 45p/disc)	£............
		Total Due	£............

Send to: P.R.M. Oliver, Nirvana, Trevingey Road Redruth, Cornwall, TR15 3DG

PLEASE NOTE
The author(s) are fully responsible for providing this Companion Disc service. The publishers of this book accept no responsibility for the supply, quality, or magnetic contents of the disc, or in respect of any damage, or injury that might be suffered or caused by its use.

Notes